DONNA K. MALTESE

overflowing
WITH
joy

PRAYERS FOR A SEASON OF ABUNDANCE

BARBOUR
PUBLISHING

Print ISBN 979-8-89151-078-4

Text originally released as *Praying Your Way to Joy*, published by Barbour Publishing.

Published by Barbour Publishing, Inc., 1810 Barbour Drive, Uhrichsville, Ohio 44683, www.barbourbooks.com

Our mission is to inspire the world with the life-changing message of the Bible.

 Member of the
Evangelical Christian
Publishers Association

Printed in China.

IF YOU'VE EVER FELT MORE JOY-LESS THAN JOY-FULL... YOU'VE COME TO THE RIGHT PLACE!

This lovely book will walk you through dozens of encouraging, inspiring, heartfelt, joy-bursting prayers that will help your beautiful soul discover true delight and contentment in an ever-growing relationship with the heavenly Father, the joy-giver Himself. Every heartfelt prayer begins with thought-provoking scripture selection and is meant to be a joyful beginning to your own personal prayer time. Joy. . .is just a prayer away!

*Be full of joy always
because you belong to the Lord.
Again I say, be full of joy!*

PHILIPPIANS 4:4 NLV

EVEN *at* NIGHT

I will give honor and thanks to the Lord, Who has told me what to do.
Yes, even at night my mind teaches me. I have placed the Lord always in
front of me. Because He is at my right hand, I will not be moved. And so
my heart is glad. My soul is full of joy. My body also will rest without fear.
PSALM 16:7–9 NLV

You, Lord, are the font of wisdom. You are the one who knows all things—even how many hairs are on my head! So I am giving honor and thanks to You. Show me which way to go, what to say, when to say it. At night, Lord, stop all those what-if thoughts from ricocheting around in my head. Replace them with Your peace and presence. With You next to me, I know nothing can shake me. I can stand in confidence and move forward in hope. You make my heart soar with gladness. You fill my soul with joy. My body relaxes in Your all-encompassing peace as I lean back upon You and rest my weary head. Amen.

ALL GOOD THINGS

Keep me, O God, for I am safe in You. I said to the Lord, "You are my Lord. All the good things I have come from You." As for those in the land who belong to You, they are the great ones in whom is all my joy.
PSALM 16:1–3 NLV

Lord, when I am alone, scared, or confused, I know I can run to You. You are the one who can protect me from all that comes against me, within and without. In You I can hide from the lure of the world. In You my soul and spirit find peace and calm. You have a way of unruffling my feathers, ever so gently. So now, in this moment, I come to rest in Your companionable light, love, and silence. Place Your hedge of protection around me, sheltering me from outside dangers and inner negative thoughts. Remind me that all the good I have in this life comes from You. Thank You, Lord, for all Your blessings upon me and for all the joy You have waiting for me as I wait on You. "You are my Lord. All the good things I have come from You." In Jesus' name, I pray, amen.

HAPPINESS FOREVER

My future is in Your hands. The land given to me is good.
Yes, my share is beautiful to me. . . . For You will not give me over
to the grave. And You will not allow Your Holy One to return
to dust. You will show me the way of life. Being with You is to
be full of joy. In Your right hand there is happiness forever.
PSALM 16:5–6, 10–11 NLV

Lord, when I'm stuck in a pattern of negative thoughts or am allowing fear to control my life, my heart races, my brow sweats, my soul despairs, and my spirit sinks. And it's all because I've somehow moved away from You; forgotten Your power, grace, mercy, strength, and help. I'm allowing everything *but You* to control me. So I'm back, Lord, remembering *You* are the one who holds my future. *You* are the one who has helped me in the past and given me all the good I have. So here I am in the present in Your presence. Here with You, I find my joy! For I know You will show me the way You would have me go, the way that leads to that happily forever after. Amen.

GIVING WAY *to* GOD

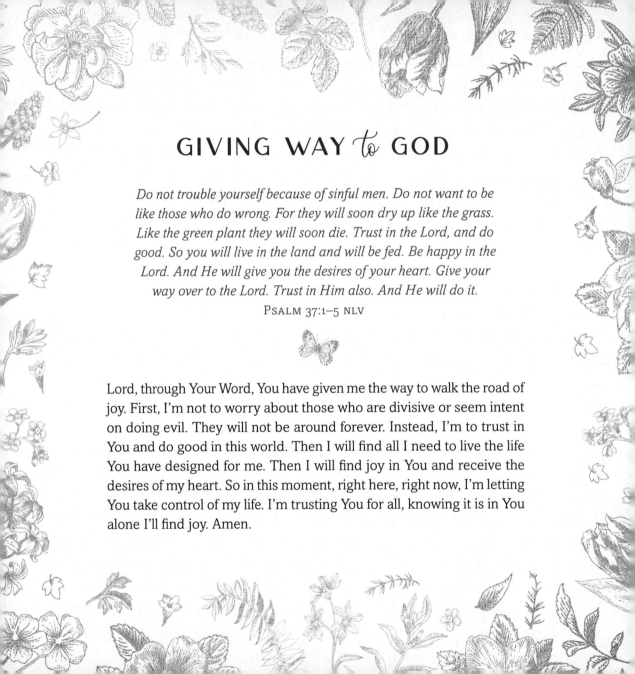

Do not trouble yourself because of sinful men. Do not want to be like those who do wrong. For they will soon dry up like the grass. Like the green plant they will soon die. Trust in the Lord, and do good. So you will live in the land and will be fed. Be happy in the Lord. And He will give you the desires of your heart. Give your way over to the Lord. Trust in Him also. And He will do it.

PSALM 37:1–5 NLV

Lord, through Your Word, You have given me the way to walk the road of joy. First, I'm not to worry about those who are divisive or seem intent on doing evil. They will not be around forever. Instead, I'm to trust in You and do good in this world. Then I will find all I need to live the life You have designed for me. Then I will find joy in You and receive the desires of my heart. So in this moment, right here, right now, I'm letting You take control of my life. I'm trusting You for all, knowing it is in You alone I'll find joy. Amen.

GREAT EXPECTATIONS

The Lord [earnestly] waits [expecting, looking, and longing] to be gracious to you; and therefore He lifts Himself up, that He may have mercy on you and show loving-kindness to you. . . . Blessed (happy, fortunate, to be envied) are all those who [earnestly] wait for Him, who expect and look and long for Him [for His victory, His favor, His love, His peace, His joy, and His matchless, unbroken companionship]!
ISAIAH 30:18 AMPC

How wonderful, Lord, that in every moment You are waiting and expecting to be gracious to me. You have scads of mercy and loving-kindness whenever I need them. So help me to be patient, Lord. Help me to drop whatever burdens I'm bearing and open up my arms to You and the blessings You have for me. My eyes are on You. I long for Your never-ending supply of strength, love, peace, and joy. I cherish and seek out Your company, Your "matchless, unbroken companionship," each and every second of my day. For I know that by returning to and resting in You, I will be saved. In quietness and trusting confidence I will find my source of strength (see Isaiah 30:15). Amen.

MORE THAN YOU NEED

Do not trouble yourself when all goes well with the one who carries out his sinful plans. Stop being angry. Turn away from fighting. Do not trouble yourself. It leads only to wrong-doing. For those who do wrong will be cut off. But those who wait for the Lord will be given the earth. . . . And they will be happy and have much more than they need.
PSALM 37:7–9, 11 NLV

Sometimes, Lord, I get so discouraged. It seems as if the people who get all the breaks are those who are *not* followers of You! It's so frustrating. But then I remember that even those who seem to have everything actually have nothing— because they don't have You. So I'm not going to worry about the ne'er-do-wells. Instead, I'm going to focus my eyes on You. I'm going to do good because I know it not only pleases You but also gives me so much joy. I'm waiting on You, Lord, following You, loving You, looking to You for everything. For when I give You my all, I get Your all. Amen.

BOLDLY BELIEVING

If you don't know what you're doing, pray to the Father. He loves to help.
You'll get his help, and won't be condescended to when you ask for it. Ask
boldly, believingly, without a second thought. People who "worry their prayers"
are like wind-whipped waves. Don't think you're going to get anything
from the Master that way, adrift at sea, keeping all your options open.
JAMES 1:5–8 MSG

Lord, I feel as if I'm sinking in a quagmire of confusion. I don't know what to do, where to go, what to say, how to proceed. Lord, help me. Show me the way to go, the path to take, the words to say. I come to You boldly, with no reservations. For I truly believe You want to help and will choose the best path for me. And I'm not going to worry about the answer You give me, wondering how this will all work out. Instead, I am going to do whatever You call me to do, knowing that whenever You're involved in my plans, You will give me what I need to see them through and lead me to a place of joy in the process. So tell me what to do, Lord. Speak. Your servant is listening. Amen.

A GRAND PLAN

I know the thoughts and plans that I have for you, says the Lord, thoughts and plans for welfare and peace and not for evil, to give you hope in your final outcome. Then you will call upon Me, and you will come and pray to Me, and I will hear and heed you. Then you will seek Me, inquire for, and require Me [as a vital necessity] and find Me when you search for Me with all your heart.

JEREMIAH 29:11–13 AMPC

I love that You have a plan for me, Lord. The fact that You even *think* of me is astounding! Sometimes I feel so lost in this world, as if I'm just one more bit of dust, unimportant, overlooked. And then I read in Your Word that if I call on You, You will bend Your ear to my lips. You'll actually *listen* to me, hear what I have to say, and move to work in my life. If I seek You with my whole self—my heart, soul, mind, and strength—and need You in every way, I *will* find You. All this is a balm for my soul and a boost to my spirit. Amen.

THE SECRET PLACE

The Lord is my light and the One Who saves me. Whom should I fear?
The Lord is the strength of my life. Of whom should I be
afraid? . . . In the day of trouble. . . In the secret place. . .He
will hide me. He will set me high upon a rock. Then my head
will be lifted up above all those around me who hate me. I will
give gifts in His holy tent with a loud voice of joy.
PSALM 27:1, 5–6 NLV

Fear can be a major killjoy, but I'm shoring up my confidence in You, Lord. You are the most powerful being in heaven and on earth. So I need not fear anything or anyone who comes against me. You, Lord, are the one who gives me the strength to stand. My faith in You gives me the confidence I need. When the trouble starts, You give me shelter. You keep me from the darkness and warm me with Your light. When I'm in Your secret place, You increase my courage. And it is there that I cry out with joy, praising You with all my heart. Thank You, Lord, for being my all in all. Amen.

A SAFE PLACE

The steps of a good man are led by the Lord. And He is happy
in his way. When he falls, he will not be thrown down, because
the Lord holds his hand. . . . For the Lord loves what is fair
and right. He does not leave the people alone who belong to
Him. . . . He. . .saves them, because they go to Him for a safe place.
PSALM 37:23–24, 28, 40 NLV

Here's one of the things I love most about You, Lord. When I follow Your way instead of my own, I am happy, full of that inner joy only You can supply, no matter what happens. Because even if I trip up, You come to my rescue. You hold my hand and pull me back up on my feet so I can start all over again. As I grow closer and closer to You, I know I'm exactly where I belong. For You promise to always be with me. You will never leave me alone because I am Your daughter, precious in Your sight. And when things go dark, when shadows chase me, I run to You, straight into Your arms, where I am not only safe but comforted and remade. Amen.

HEART STRONG

*You have been my Helper. . . . For my father and my mother have
left me. But the Lord will take care of me. . . . I would have been
without hope if I had not believed that I would see the loving-
kindness of the Lord in the land of the living. Wait for the Lord.
Be strong. Let your heart be strong. Yes, wait for the Lord.*
PSALM 27:9–10, 13–14 NLV

Sometimes even when I'm surrounded by lots of people, I can feel
all alone. I am out of step with them because I'm so in step with You,
Lord. Yet strangely enough, it's in those times that I feel even closer to
You. Because I know that no matter who I lose, I'll always have You.
You are the helper I crave to be with. You are the one who has taken
care of me in the past, is doing so in the present, and will continue
to do so in the future. This truth gives me hope and revives my joy.
For I know I'll see Your loving-kindness here and now. Meanwhile,
I wait, knowing that as I do, You are keeping my heart and spirit
strong. Amen.

REQUEST GRANTED

Jabez was honorable above his brothers; but his mother named him
Jabez [sorrow maker], saying, Because I bore him in pain. Jabez cried
to the God of Israel, saying, Oh, that You would bless me and enlarge
my border, and that Your hand might be with me, and You would keep
me from evil so it might not hurt me! And God granted his request.

1 CHRONICLES 4:9–10 AMPC

I thank You, Lord, that You have provided me with the gift and tool of prayer. No matter how I am seen or labeled in this world, by praying to You, I can change the conversation, within and without. Although my name is not Sorrow Maker, I ask You, Lord, for Your many blessings. I ask that You would increase what I already have. That Your hand would be with me to protect me. That You would keep me from evil so I am not hurt. That You would fill my head with good thoughts. That You would open my mind and heart to Your Word, allowing it to change me from the inside out for Your glory alone. In Jesus' name, I pray, amen.

STRENGTHENED *with* TRUST

*The village. . . .had been burned to the ground, and their wives,
sons, and daughters all taken prisoner. David and his men burst
out in loud wails—wept and wept until they were exhausted with
weeping. . . . There was talk among the men, bitter over the loss of their
families, of stoning him. David strengthened himself with trust in his
G*OD*. . . . Then David prayed to G*OD*. . . . David recovered the whole lot.*
1 SAMUEL 30:3–4, 6, 8, 19 MSG

Your Word makes clear, Lord, that there are times when it's okay to
have a good cry. I should take time to mourn over the losses I suffer in
this world. After all, Jesus cried, so why not me? Yet when I'm all cried
out, I need to seek Your face so I can find my way out of any why-me
conundrums. I garner strength and encouragement by sitting in Your
presence. Then I am to pray, asking You what I should do to find a path
to restoration. Only when I have received Your instruction am I to take
the next steps. For only with Your power can I live out Your plan and
be restored to joy once more. Amen.

NEVERTHELESS

The king and his men went to Jerusalem against the Jebusites,
the inhabitants of the land, who said to David, "You will not come
in here, but the blind and the lame will ward you off"—thinking,
"David cannot come in here." Nevertheless, David took the stronghold
of Zion, that is, the city of David. . . . And David became greater
*and greater, for the L*ORD*, the God of hosts, was with him.*

2 SAMUEL 5:6–7, 10 ESV

Every success David had, Lord, was because You were with him—*and* David was with You. That's how I want to live my life, Lord. When You call me to do something, when You want me to follow in Jesus' steps and to live out what You have planned for me, I do not want to be dissuaded or discouraged by what other people say. I want to *nevertheless* take the strongholds You want me to take. Win the battles You want me to win. For then, not only will I have the joy of that success, but You will take joy in me as well. Give me that courage, Lord. Be with me in all You would have me do. Help me to live a nevertheless life for Your glory. Amen.

SAVING POWER

"The Lord says to you, 'Do not be afraid or troubled because of
these many men. For the battle is not yours but God's. Go down to
fight them tomorrow. . . . You will not need to fight in this battle.
Just stand still in your places and see the saving power of the
Lord work for you, O Judah and Jerusalem.' Do not be afraid or
troubled. Go out against them tomorrow, for the Lord is with you."
2 CHRONICLES 20:15–17 NLV

Lord, when forces come up against me, I so often try to fight them on my own, in my own strength, and according to my own game plan. Yet Your Word makes it clear that the very first thing I should do when I'm in trouble is come to You, praising You and thanking You for all the ways You provide for me and work in my life. Then I am to ask what I should do—if I should stand still and watch You fight for me or move out and face my foe with Your strength and courage running through me, knowing that in the end, whatever the result, I *will* rejoice in Your saving power. Amen.

THE POWER of PRAISE

"Trust in the Lord your God, and you will be made strong. Trust in the men who speak for Him, and you will do well." . . . [Jehoshaphat] called those who sang to the Lord and those who praised Him in holy clothing. They went out in front of the army and said, "Give thanks to the Lord. For His loving-kindness lasts forever." When they began to sing and praise, the Lord set traps against the men.

2 CHRONICLES 20:20–22 NLV

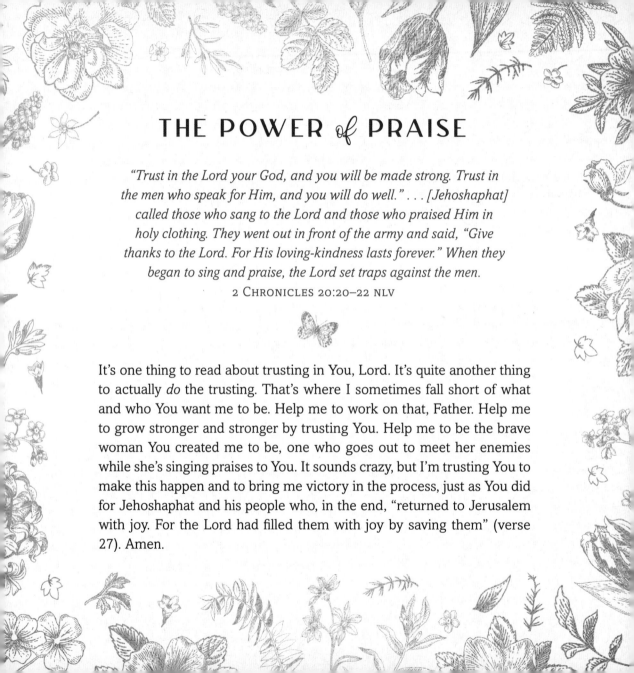

It's one thing to read about trusting in You, Lord. It's quite another thing to actually *do* the trusting. That's where I sometimes fall short of what and who You want me to be. Help me to work on that, Father. Help me to grow stronger and stronger by trusting You. Help me to be the brave woman You created me to be, one who goes out to meet her enemies while she's singing praises to You. It sounds crazy, but I'm trusting You to make this happen and to bring me victory in the process, just as You did for Jehoshaphat and his people who, in the end, "returned to Jerusalem with joy. For the Lord had filled them with joy by saving them" (verse 27). Amen.

HAPPY *for* HOPE

Now that we have been made right with God by putting our trust in Him, we have peace with Him. It is because of what our Lord Jesus Christ did for us. By putting our trust in God, He has given us His loving-favor and has received us. We are happy for the hope we have of sharing the shining-greatness of God. We are glad for our troubles also. We know that troubles help us learn not to give up.

ROMANS 5:1–3 NLV

Oh Lord Jesus, thank You for loving me so much that You died to save my soul. You did this to make me right with God so that I can have access to Him through prayer and praises. This gives me such peace. It's clear I cannot make it through this life without You by my side, without looking to You for an example of what I am to do and say. Now, as I trust God with all my heart, soul, mind, and strength, I can have joy no matter what my situation. No matter what troubles come against me, I will never give up, for I have hope, knowing You will help me through thick and thin, life and death. Amen.

GOD'S BLESSINGS

You shall keep the Feast of Weeks to the Lord your God with a tribute
of a freewill offering from your hand, which you shall give to the Lord
your God, as the Lord your God blesses you. . . . You shall rejoice in your
Feast. . . because the Lord your God will bless you in all your produce
and in all the works of your hands, so that you will be altogether joyful.
DEUTERONOMY 16:10, 14–15 AMPC

I can't remember the last time I came to You with nothing but praise and thanks, Lord, for all the ways You've blessed me. Instead, I seem to mostly either unload my troubles or ask You for things. So today, Lord, I come to You wanting nothing, only giving You thanks. Thank You for saving me, loving me, protecting me, and watching over me. Thank You for the food, clothing, and shelter You so adequately provide. Thank You for blessings seen and unseen. And thank You for blessing the work I put my hands to, so that I can be "altogether joyful." What a great God You are! All praise and glory to You, dear Lord. Amen.

MORNING MOMENTS

In the morning You hear my voice, O Lord; in the morning I prepare
[a prayer, a sacrifice] for You and watch and wait [for You to
speak to my heart]. . . . Let all those who take refuge and put their
trust in You rejoice; let them ever sing and shout for joy, because
You make a covering over them and defend them; let those also
who love Your name be joyful in You and be in high spirits.
PSALM 5:3, 11 AMPC

In these early morning moments, Lord, I come to You. Hear my voice.
I'm giving You my all—my heart, soul, body, and mind. I await Your
presence. Come to me, Lord. Speak gently, softly, to my heart. Tell me
the words You want me to hear as I take refuge in You, laying down all
my burdens and taking up Your strength, courage, and love. Fill me with
Your Spirit. Shield me from any dangers that may come. Help me to stay
attuned to You all through this day. Lord, I love You ever so much, to the
moon and back and more. For it is with and in You that I find my true
joy every moment of the day. Amen.

SINGING *and* DANCING

David went everywhere that Saul sent him, and did well. Saul had him lead the men of war. And it was pleasing to all the people and to Saul's servants. When David returned from killing the Philistine, the women came out of all the cities of Israel, singing and dancing, to meet King Saul, playing songs of joy on timbrels. The women sang as they played, and said, "Saul has killed his thousands, and David his ten thousands."

1 SAMUEL 18:5–7 NLV

It's so easy to cheer for and celebrate people who play sports or act on the stage or screen. But when it comes to celebrating You, Lord, I seem to hesitate, wondering what people will think of me. Help me to change that up, dear God. I want to be like the women who sang and danced with abandon back in David's day. For doing so not only pleases You but fills me with such joy, lifting me higher in mind, spirit, and body. It's a win-win for both of us, Lord. So I come to You with abandon today, dancing as I sing my song of praise just for You! Amen.

TURNED HEARTS

They finished their building by decree of the God of Israel and by decree of Cyrus and Darius and Artaxerxes king of Persia. . . . And the people of Israel. . .celebrated the dedication of this house of God with joy. . . . For the LORD had made them joyful and had turned the heart of the king of Assyria to them, so that he aided them in the work of the house of God.

 EZRA 6:14, 16, 22 ESV

Only You, Lord, have the power to turn the hearts of rulers, whether they be queens, presidents, tyrants, or dictators, so that Your work can be accomplished through them and us. This gives me hope that You can turn even the most godless person to help Your people do what You have called them to do, no matter how great the task. And that hope in You and Your power working to change people, against all odds and appearances to the contrary, gives me great joy. For with You, nothing is impossible. In Your power I not only rest but go forward with confidence, hope, and joy. In Jesus' name, amen.

HEALING POWER

A gentle tongue [with its healing power] is a tree of life. . . . A man has joy in making an apt answer, and a word spoken at the right moment—how good it is! . . . The mind of the [uncompromisingly] righteous studies how to answer. . . . The light in the eyes [of him whose heart is joyful] rejoices the hearts of others, and good news nourishes the bones.

PROVERBS 15:4, 23, 28, 30 AMPC

Lord, please reign over and rein in my tongue. There are so many times I speak without thinking and end up hurting others. I want to follow the steps of Christ, Lord—to build people up, not tear them down. So help me, Lord, to have a gentle tongue that heals others so they can grow closer to You. Show me how to increase the joys of others with a balm, not destroy them with a bomb. Help me to study how to answer before I speak and to think before I let one word cross my lips. For then not only I but those with whom I speak will be filled with joy. Amen.

A GLAD HEART

A glad heart makes a cheerful countenance, but by sorrow of heart the spirit is broken. . . . All the days of the desponding and afflicted are made evil [by anxious thoughts and forebodings], but he who has a glad heart has a continual feast [regardless of circumstances]. Better is little with the reverent, worshipful fear of the Lord than great and rich treasure and trouble with it.

PROVERBS 15:13, 15–16 AMPC

Abba, some days I find myself brought so low by what's happening in the world. And sometimes my chin is on the floor because of what's happening in my home, my family, or my work. More often than not, my mind is filled with anxious thoughts and forebodings. But I don't want to live that way. I want to have a glad heart—no matter what's happening. So I need Your help to focus on the good things, the things above, not the things of this earth. Help me, Lord, not to worry about anything—money, relationships, wars, or other troubles—but to keep my chin up by keeping my eyes and focus on You alone. In Jesus' name, amen.

RISING UP *to the* LOVE

Arise, my love, my fair one, and come away. [So I went with him, and when we were climbing the rocky steps up the hillside, my beloved shepherd said to me] O my dove, [while you are here]. . . in the sheltered and secret place of the cliff, let me see your face, let me hear your voice; for your voice is sweet, and your face is lovely. [My heart was touched and I fervently sang to him my desire].

SONG OF SOLOMON 2:13–15 AMPC

It fills me with joy, Lord, that You call me "my love." That You want me to come away with You to that secret place where we meet, just You and me alone. That You want to see my face and hear my voice. That You think I'm lovely. Thank You, my beloved, for calling me to rise up to You and tell You about my desires and all the things that are on my heart. There is nothing and no one like You, Lord. To You alone I bear all my secrets, all my longings, knowing that You will not laugh at them but will treasure them. Dear heart, I love You. Amen.

A HEART AWAKE

I went to sleep, but my heart stayed awake. [I dreamed that I heard] the voice of my beloved as he knocked [at the door of my mother's cottage]. Open to me, my sister, my love, my dove, my spotless one [he said]. . . . [But weary from a day in the vineyards, I had already sought my rest] I had put off my garment—how could I [again] put it on? I had washed my feet—how could I [again] soil them?
SONG OF SOLOMON 5:2–3 AMPC

Lord, in Your presence I experience such unfathomable joy. Yet at times I am so worn out from earthly cares that I do not open my door to You. In those moments I miss out on Your peace, calm, wisdom, power, strength, and gentle touch. Even in the night hours, asleep or awake, I want to be available to You—to Your voice, Your whisper, Your knock upon my door. Help me to keep attuned to Your quest for me. May my spirit be so linked to Yours that I don't know where I stop and You begin. I pray this in Jesus' precious name, amen.

JOYFULLY RADIANT

[She proudly said] I am my beloved's, and his desire is toward me!
. . . Many waters cannot quench love, neither can floods drown
it. . . . [Joyfully the radiant bride turned to him, the one altogether
lovely, the chief among ten thousand to her soul, and with unconcealed
eagerness to begin her life of sweet companionship with him,
she answered] Make haste, my beloved, and come quickly, like a
gazelle or a young hart [and take me to our waiting home].
SONG OF SOLOMON 7:10; 8:7, 14 AMPC

The fact that You desire me, Lord, fills me with such delight. I rejoice
that I am Yours and You are mine and that the love we have for each
other can never disappear. I am so eager to turn to You, to begin our
life together each morning. Take me to that rock that is higher than I,
that secret place where it is only You and me, together forever. That is
my true home, my true abode where nothing untoward can touch me
and where You cover me with Your love. You dry my tears and simply
hold me, telling me all is well and will be well. You are my heaven on
earth. Amen.

BEYOND UNDERSTANDING

*Be full of joy always because you belong to the Lord. Again I
say, be full of joy! Let all people see how gentle you are. . . . Do
not worry. Learn to pray about everything. Give thanks to God
as you ask Him for what you need. The peace of God is much
greater than the human mind can understand. This peace
will keep your hearts and minds through Christ Jesus.*
PHILIPPIANS 4:4–7 NLV

Joy, at times, seems elusive, Lord. But that's only because I forget to
call on You, my champion, my master, my Creator, the all-powerful
one who makes the seemingly impossible possible! Instead of running to You, I let my worries begin a running dialogue in my head.
Soon they spin out of control and build up to a sort of mild panic.
Help me, Lord, to learn to pray about anything and everything—and
to thank You in the process. For Your Word says that if I do, Your
peace beyond understanding will surround me and guard me. So
here I am, Lord, telling You all, thanking You for all. . . . Ah, now it's
time to rejoice! Amen.

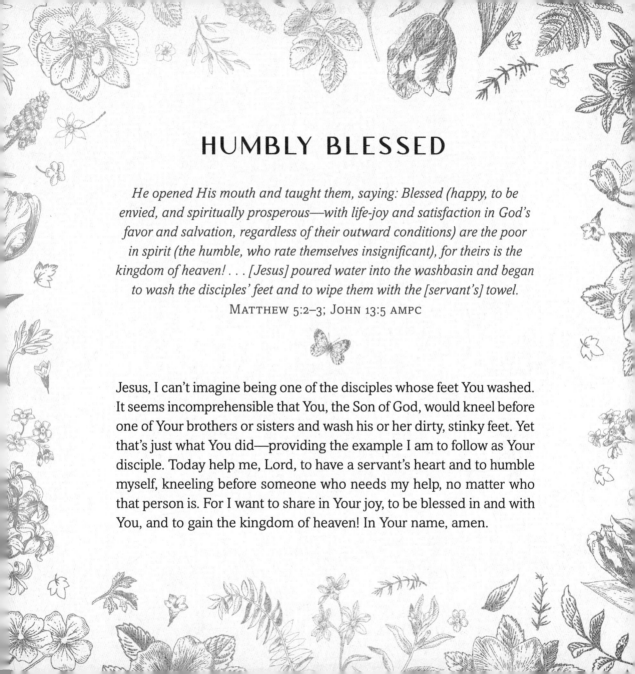

HUMBLY BLESSED

He opened His mouth and taught them, saying: Blessed (happy, to be envied, and spiritually prosperous—with life-joy and satisfaction in God's favor and salvation, regardless of their outward conditions) are the poor in spirit (the humble, who rate themselves insignificant), for theirs is the kingdom of heaven! . . . [Jesus] poured water into the washbasin and began to wash the disciples' feet and to wipe them with the [servant's] towel.

MATTHEW 5:2–3; JOHN 13:5 AMPC

Jesus, I can't imagine being one of the disciples whose feet You washed. It seems incomprehensible that You, the Son of God, would kneel before one of Your brothers or sisters and wash his or her dirty, stinky feet. Yet that's just what You did—providing the example I am to follow as Your disciple. Today help me, Lord, to have a servant's heart and to humble myself, kneeling before someone who needs my help, no matter who that person is. For I want to share in Your joy, to be blessed in and with You, and to gain the kingdom of heaven! In Your name, amen.

WORDS *of* JOY

O Lord, You know and understand; [earnestly] remember me and visit me and avenge me on my persecutors. Take me not away [from joy or from life itself] in Your long-suffering [to my enemies]; know that for Your sake I suffer and bear reproach. Your words were found, and I ate them; and Your words were to me a joy and the rejoicing of my heart, for I am called by Your name, O Lord God of hosts.

JEREMIAH 15:15–16 AMPC

God, I am so glad You can see what I'm going through, all the things I'm up against. You know how my troubles are zapping my joy. But then I reach for Your Word. I open Your Book and discover You. Letter by letter, word by word, sentence by sentence, I absorb all You have to say to me—how You love and work with me, how You want all that is good to come to me. You even have a plan for me. And it is here, within Your Word and presence, that I find the joy I need to live this life. Thank You for allowing me to hear Your voice and find my way home to You. Amen.

MIND OVER MATTERS

Keep your minds thinking about whatever is true, whatever is respected, whatever is right, whatever is pure, whatever can be loved, and whatever is well thought of. If there is anything good and worth giving thanks for, think about these things. Keep on doing all the things you learned and received and heard from me. Do the things you saw me do. Then the God Who gives peace will be with you.
PHILIPPIANS 4:8–9 NLV

Too often, Lord, I find myself so engrossed in the bad things happening in the world that I forget about all the good that surrounds me—You and Your Word included. So help me to lift my thoughts in Your direction, Lord. I want to fill my mind with and meditate on things that are good, true, and uplifting. I want to think the best, not the worst; to think of the lovely, not the unlovely. I want to think of things to praise, not things to criticize. But I need Your help. Make it my desire, Lord, to fill my mind with You before I reach for the paper or turn on the news. For I know that if I'm full of You and Your goodness, I won't have room for anything else—but joy. Amen.

GLAD *in* GOD

I'm glad in God, far happier than you would ever guess. . . . I don't have a sense of needing anything personally. I've learned by now to be quite content whatever my circumstances. I'm just as happy with little as with much, with much as with little. I've found the recipe for being happy whether full or hungry, hands full or hands empty. Whatever I have, wherever I am, I can make it through anything in the One who makes me who I am.

PHILIPPIANS 4:10–13 MSG

So many people are miserable, Lord. They are always in a state of wanting, never quite feeling complete and happy. I must admit that sometimes I find myself there too. I am envious of others and what they have and can do. But then I think of You and all those desires fade. I find myself quite content, even happy with what I have and what's happening in my life. For You, Lord, are all I need. With You giving me strength, grace, mercy, love, hope, and so much more, I'm happy whether my pantry is full or empty, my house warm or cold, my bank balance abundant or sparse. I'm at peace and glad in You. Amen.

TENDER TEARS *of* LOVE

He opened His mouth and taught them, saying: . . . Blessed and
enviably happy [with a happiness produced by the experience of God's
favor and especially conditioned by the revelation of His matchless
grace] are those who mourn, for they shall be comforted! . . . He
said, Where have you laid him? They said to Him, Lord, come and
see. Jesus wept. The Jews said, See how [tenderly] He loved him!
MATTHEW 5:2, 4; JOHN 11:34–36 AMPC

You, Jesus, are well aware of all the sorrows I have suffered, for You
Yourself are called "a Man of sorrows and pains, and acquainted with
grief" (Isaiah 53:3 AMPC). When You were looking for Your friend Lazarus,
knowing he had died, You wept tears of tender pity and love. Yet You
have taught that even in my sorrows, I can find joy. For You, who know
what I've gone through, will comfort me. And it is that comfort I seek
now. Be with me, Lord. Wipe away my tears. Hold me in Your arms
until I once again experience gladness in You. Amen.

A QUIET STRENGTH

Blessed (happy, blithesome, joyous, spiritually prosperous—with life-joy and satisfaction in God's favor and salvation, regardless of their outward conditions) are the meek (the mild, patient, long-suffering), for they shall inherit the earth! . . . Say to the Daughter of Zion. . . Behold, your King is coming to you, lowly and riding on a donkey, and on a colt, the foal of a donkey [a beast of burden].
MATTHEW 5:5; 21:5 AMPC

When I think about it, it doesn't seem like I'd be very happy being meek, Jesus. Yet that is what You were and what You've called me to be. When I look to You as my example, I realize being meek doesn't mean being weak. It means being obedient to Abba God. Trusting Him to handle what I cannot. Being quiet and patient while He works out His will and way. And being gentle with others. In this view, being meek carries strength with it. You Yourself, the Son of God and my King, rode a simple donkey through the throng the Sunday before Your death. I want to have that meekness, that trust in Abba God. Show me the way there so that I too can find the joy that comes with quiet strength. Amen.

A PEACEFUL SLEEP

When you are on your bed, look into your hearts and be quiet. Give the
gifts that are right and good, and trust in the Lord. Many are asking,
"Who will show us any good?" . . . You have filled my heart with
more happiness than they have when there is much grain and wine.
I will lie down and sleep in peace. O Lord, You alone keep me safe.
PSALM 4:4–8 NLV

It's so hard to have joy, Lord, when I don't get enough sleep at night.
So I'm asking for Your help. When I'm in bed, help me to commune with
my heart. To review my day and ask Your forgiveness for anything I may
have done or said that I shouldn't have. To count my blessings, one by
one. Then, Lord, help me to quiet my body and soul in Your presence.
Fill me with all the joy I need to find peace of heart and mind. For only
then, with You and Your blessings covering me, with Your protection
and arms around me, will I find the rest I need and the safety I crave.
In Jesus' name, I pray, amen.

SPIRITUAL NOURISHMENT

He opened His mouth and taught them, saying: . . . Blessed and fortunate and happy and spiritually prosperous (in that state in which the born-again child of God enjoys His favor and salvation) are those who hunger and thirst for righteousness (uprightness and right standing with God), for they shall be completely satisfied! . . . The disciples urged Him saying, Rabbi, eat something. But He assured them, I have food (nourishment) to eat of which you know nothing and have no idea.

MATTHEW 5:2, 6; JOHN 4:31–32 AMPC

Abba God, only You can fill this longing I have inside, this God-shaped hole within me. I ache to hear Your voice, see Your face, feel Your touch. I hunger and thirst for all You have to give me, for all You are holding for me. I know You're just waiting to give me everything I need. So help me, Lord, to let go of all things that are not of You—worries, fears, and what-ifs; possessions, deadlines, stress, and anxieties. For when I empty myself of all but You and Your Word, I know I'll find the nourishment that brings with it all the joy my spirit craves. Amen.

REVIVED AGAIN

Be to me a rock of refuge, to which I may continually come. . . . O God, from my youth you have taught me, and I still proclaim your wondrous deeds. So even to old age and gray hairs, O God, do not forsake me, until I proclaim your might to another generation. . . . You. . .will revive me again. . . . My lips will shout for joy, when I sing praises to you.
PSALM 71:3, 17–18, 20, 23 ESV

You have never failed me, Lord. When I've needed Your help, You have always come through for me. Time and time again, You have worked wonders in my life. Since I was a child in the faith, You have been my rock of refuge. So do not leave me now, Lord. Help me to grow more and more like Your Son, Jesus. Give me the words to tell others of Your power, love, compassion, and strength. Renew me. Fill me with Your light. Work in me for Your good and glory. And I will shout for joy as I sing Your praises. Amen.

NEVER FORGOTTEN

Sing for joy, O heavens! Be glad, O earth! Break out into songs of joy,
O mountains! For the Lord has comforted His people. . . . "Can a woman
forget her nursing child? Can she have no pity on the son to whom she
gave birth? Even these may forget, but I will not forget you. See, I have
marked your names on My hands. Your walls are always before Me."
ISAIAH 49:13, 15–16 NLV

Oh Lord, with You in my life, I need not worry about being passed
over! For You are always with me. You will never forget me—just like a
nursing mother will never forget her newborn. But You go even further
by tattooing my name on Your hands! Thank You for leading me, protecting me before and behind, providing for me, healing me, showering
me with blessings, and fighting those who threaten me. Your pervading
presence in my life gives me such joy. Such peace of mind. Thank You,
Father God, for never leaving me behind. Because of You, I break out,
singing songs of joy. In Jesus' name, I praise You, amen.

LOVING CARE NOT SPARED

*He opened His mouth and taught them, saying: . . . Blessed
(happy, to be envied, and spiritually prosperous—with life-joy
and satisfaction in God's favor and salvation, regardless of their
outward conditions) are the merciful, for they shall obtain mercy!
. . . As Jesus passed on from there, two blind men followed Him,
shouting loudly, Have pity and mercy on us, Son of David!
. . . Then He touched their eyes. . .and their eyes were opened.*
MATTHEW 5:2, 7; 9:27, 29–30 AMPC

I thank You, Jesus, for Your mercy. Your loving-kindness and Your care
for me seem to have no end. While You were here on earth, You were
constantly reaching out to help others. And Your Word tells me that if I
am kind and loving to others, caring for them as You care for me, I will
find myself loved and cared for. So, Lord, help me to reach out in love
to those who need it. To care for those who are burdened. For when I
do, the blessings and joy will flow, eyes will be opened, and hearts will
be touched for You. In Jesus' name, amen.

PURE LIGHT *and* JOY

You are the Lord Most High over all the earth. . . . Let those who love the Lord hate what is bad. For He keeps safe the souls of His faithful ones. He takes them away from the hand of the sinful. Light is spread like seed for those who are right and good, and joy for the pure in heart. Be glad in the Lord, you who are right and good. Give thanks to His holy name.
PSALM 97:9–12 NLV

Lord, help my love of You keep me away from things that are not good for me. For anything that is not good is not of You, God. Keep my soul safe from the evil that presents itself in the physical and spiritual worlds. Hide me under Your banner of love so that the sinful cannot reach me. Shine Your light along my way so that I will not stumble upon Your path. Help me to continue to walk in Jesus' steps, the right and good way, for there alone will I find the deep joy I seek and the pure love I crave from You. In Jesus' name, I pray, amen.

OPEN DOORS

*Though the disciples were behind closed doors for fear of the Jews,
Jesus came and stood among them and said, Peace to you! So saying,
He showed them His hands and His side. And when the disciples saw
the Lord, they were filled with joy (delight, exultation, ecstasy, rapture).
Then Jesus said to them again, Peace to you! . . . And having said this,
He breathed on them and said to them, Receive the Holy Spirit!*
JOHN 20:19–22 AMPC

Lord Jesus, sometimes this world leaves me cowering in fear, afraid to move forward. In defense, I put up walls and barriers, hoping my safety will lie there. But You, Lord, open all doors and come shining through. Your words and Your blessing of peace draw me out of my fear and into You. Seeing Your face, I am filled with joy once more. Reminded of who You are, what You've suffered for me, I am renewed, made whole again. Your peace and Spirit surround me, cocooning me in Your grace, mercy, love, and presence. Breathe on me, Jesus. Strengthen my heart, soul, and mind as I abide and rest in You. Amen.

BLESSINGS *of* GOODNESS

The king shall have joy in Your strength, O LORD; and in Your salvation how greatly shall he rejoice! You have given him his heart's desire, and have not withheld the request of his lips. For You meet him with the blessings of goodness. . . . You have made him exceedingly glad with Your presence. For the king trusts in the LORD, and through the mercy of the Most High he shall not be moved.

PSALM 21:1–3, 6–7 NKJV

It's Your strength and power, Lord, that get me through each day, that bring me great joy. Every day You shower me with blessings, giving me what I desire, answering my prayers. All that is good comes from Your hand. And for all these things I thank You, Lord. Yet no blessing, no good thing You place in my life gives me more joy than Your very presence. For it is my trust that You will come when I call, my faith that You are here by my side right now, and my belief in Your loving-kindness that keep me steady, able to walk, able to serve You. In Jesus' name, amen.

PURE HEART VISION

He opened His mouth and taught them, saying: . . . Blessed (happy,
enviably fortunate, and spiritually prosperous. . .) are the pure
in heart, for they shall see God! . . . No man has ever seen God
at any time; the only unique Son. . .Who is in the bosom [in the
intimate presence] of the Father, He has declared Him [He has
revealed Him and brought Him out where He can be seen].
MATTHEW 5:2, 8; JOHN 1:18 AMPC

Only by looking at and through You, Jesus, can I see God in all His
goodness, strength, power, mercy, and loving-kindness. Yet to be able
to see God completely, to actually be able to fully enter into His presence, my heart and mind must be right with You. So help me, Lord,
to get and keep my heart pure. Help me to focus my thoughts on You,
Jesus. To steep myself in Your Word. To walk in Your way. To stay on
Your path. To forgive as You have forgiven. And to follow Your lead in
all I do and say, all I think and pray. In Your name, amen.

ROAD TO WISDOM

Trust in the Lord with all your heart, and do not trust in your own understanding. Agree with Him in all your ways, and He will make your paths straight. Do not be wise in your own eyes. Fear the Lord and turn away from what is sinful. It will be healing to your body and medicine to your bones. . . . Happy is the man who finds wisdom, and the man who gets understanding.

PROVERBS 3:5–8, 13 NLV

This world seems to be getting more and more complicated every day. There are so many choices one can make, so many roads one can take. I'm sometimes confused, Lord, not sure what to do, which path to choose. Give me the wisdom I need to walk the right way. I'm trusting You and Your wisdom, not my own. I'm going to agree with You on everything. I'm turning myself over to You, knowing that in Your wisdom lies my path to true and lasting joy. Under Your direction will I find the true remedy I need. Amen.

LOOKING *at* YOU

"O give thanks to the Lord. Call upon His name. Let the people know what He has done. Sing to Him. Sing praises to Him. Tell of all His great works. Have joy in His holy name. Let the heart of those who look to the Lord be glad. Look to the Lord and ask for His strength. Look to Him all the time. Remember His great works which He has done."
1 CHRONICLES 16:8–12 NLV

Today, Lord, I want to thank You for calling me. I praise Your name in remembrance of all You have done for Your people—from parting the Red Sea, to making the earth stand still, to sending a host of angels to protect us, to sending Your Son to bring us back to You, heart, body, mind, and soul. You have breathed Your life into me, Lord. And to You, my source, I look at all times—for guidance, protection, love, mercy, forgiveness, strength, and power. In Your name and works, in Your lovely face, I find all the joy I desire. Here's looking at You, Lord, today and forever. Amen.

NEVER SEEN, YET BELIEVED

His disciples were again in the house, and Thomas was with them.
Jesus came, though they were behind closed doors, and stood
among them and said, Peace to you! . . . Because you have seen
Me, Thomas, do you now believe (trust, have faith)? Blessed and
happy and to be envied are those who have never seen Me and
yet have believed and adhered to and trusted and relied on Me.
JOHN 20:26, 29 AMPC

It's true, Jesus. I have never seen You physically. Yet unlike doubting Thomas, I believe in You. Between You and me are no closed doors. As soon as You stand beside me, I feel Your peace and joy, Your strength and power. You call me blessed and happy because I believe in, rely on, and trust in You without ever having seen You. And I *am*! For You are my way to the Father. You are the truth I need. You are the life I seek. I am nowhere without You. So stick close to me, Lord, as I stick close to You. Continually bless me as I follow in Your footsteps. Help me to recognize that no matter what each day brings, my path, my purpose, and my joy lie in You. Amen.

LIFTING UP

I will lift You up, O Lord, for You have lifted me up. You have not let those who hate me stand over me in joy. O Lord my God, I cried to You for help and You healed me. O Lord, You have brought me up from the grave. You have kept me alive, so that I will not go down into the deep. Sing praise to the Lord, all you who belong to Him. Give thanks to His holy name.

PSALM 30:1–4 NLV

It's only right that I should lift You up, Lord, because You've certainly lifted me up. When I first awoke, I wondered what this day would bring. But before my thoughts went too far, I looked to You and into Your Word. There I found how You continually help and heal me. You give me new life each and every day. You and Your light are what keep me from sliding into that dark abyss. So today, Lord, I'm praising Your name, singing songs of love to You. I thank You for always being there; rescuing me when I'm in danger; walking with me through the storms; holding me tight in the night hours; showing me the pathway of life. . .in You. Amen.

SWIMMING *in* SUCCESS

Simon Peter said to them, "I am going fishing." The others said,
"We will go with you.". . . That night they caught no fish. Early in
the morning Jesus stood on the shore of the lake. . . . He said to
them, "Put your net over the right side of the boat. Then you will
catch some fish." They put out the net. They were not able to pull
it in because it was so full of fish. . . . There were 153 big fish.
JOHN 21:3–4, 6, 11 NLV

Jesus, I love this story of how Your discouraged disciples have caught
no fish. Then You come along, tell them what to do, and they end up
catching 153! But the best part is that when Peter realizes it's You,
he jumps into the water and swims to Your side! What an expression
of joy! That's how I feel, Lord. When I'm discouraged, stuck, out of
ideas, Your voice comes through. I follow it, and the next thing I know,
I'm swimming in success, rushing joyfully to Your side to share my
bounty with You! Thank You, Lord, for all the victories You supply,
to Your glory. In Jesus' name, I pray, amen.

DRESSED *with* JOY

Sing praise to the Lord, all you who belong to Him. . . . His favor is for life. Crying may last for a night, but joy comes with the new day. . . . Show me loving-kindness. O Lord, be my Helper. You have turned my crying into dancing. You have taken off my clothes made from hair, and dressed me with joy. So my soul may sing praise to You, and not be quiet.

PSALM 30:4–5, 10–12 NLV

Sometimes, Lord, when I'm grieving over a loss, it's hard to even consider happiness. Yet a seed of joy can be found in the hope of Your Word. For You have said, "Crying may last for a night, but joy comes with the new day." On the down days, Lord, help me to tap into that hope, that promise that someday, at some point, I will once again find and experience joy. That You will turn my crying into dancing, take off my black mourning suit and dress me with joy. In the meantime, help me to write this promise on my heart so that I can in some way bring this knowledge to mind when needed and praise You amid the pain. Amen.

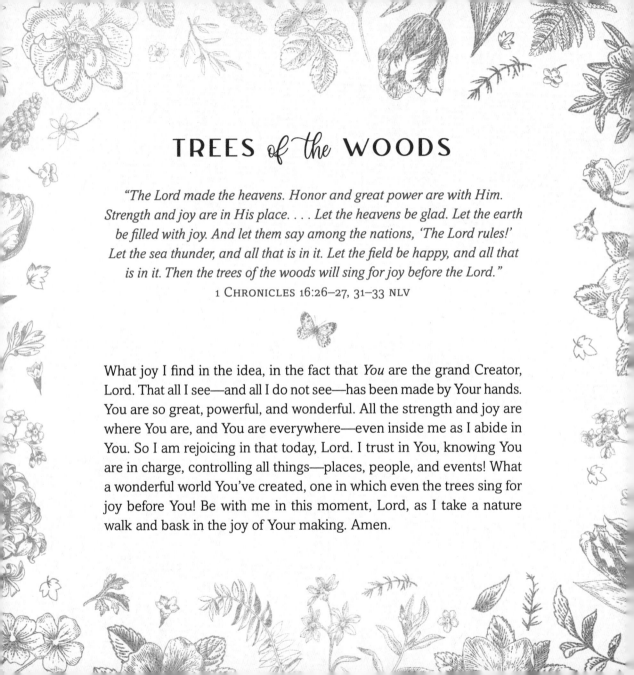

TREES *of the* WOODS

"The Lord made the heavens. Honor and great power are with Him.
Strength and joy are in His place. . . . Let the heavens be glad. Let the earth
be filled with joy. And let them say among the nations, 'The Lord rules!'
Let the sea thunder, and all that is in it. Let the field be happy, and all that
is in it. Then the trees of the woods will sing for joy before the Lord."
1 CHRONICLES 16:26–27, 31–33 NLV

What joy I find in the idea, in the fact that *You* are the grand Creator, Lord. That all I see—and all I do not see—has been made by Your hands. You are so great, powerful, and wonderful. All the strength and joy are where You are, and You are everywhere—even inside me as I abide in You. So I am rejoicing in that today, Lord. I trust in You, knowing You are in charge, controlling all things—places, people, and events! What a wonderful world You've created, one in which even the trees sing for joy before You! Be with me in this moment, Lord, as I take a nature walk and bask in the joy of Your making. Amen.

BLESSED BELIEF

*[Elizabeth] exclaimed. . .Blessed (happy, to be envied) is she who
believed that there would be a fulfillment of the things that were
spoken to her from the Lord. And Mary said, My soul magnifies
and extols the Lord, and my spirit rejoices in God my Savior,
for He has looked upon the low station and humiliation of His
handmaiden. . . . For He Who is almighty has done great things for me.*
LUKE 1:42, 45–49 AMPC

I find my strength and joy, Lord, when I believe that You will do what
Your Word says, when I have faith that You will keep Your promises to
those who love You. Help me to build up that belief and faith, Lord, more
and more each day. Remind me each and every moment that through
Your Word, strength, and power, I will not just find my way through this
life, but my soul and spirit will rejoice over You in good times and not-
so-good times. Help me to base my life on the fact that You are doing
great things for me and in me. In Jesus' name and power, I pray, amen.

THE WAY *to* WISDOM

*Happy is the man who finds wisdom, and the man who gets
understanding. . . . She is worth more than stones of great worth.
Nothing you can wish for compares with her. Long life is in her right
hand. Riches and honor are in her left hand. Her ways are pleasing,
and all her paths are peace. . . . Happy are all who hold her near.*
PROVERBS 3:13–18 NLV

I want to search out Your knowledge, Lord. To understand what
You want me to do, say, and think. Show me the path toward Your
wisdom. May I pray for that more than anything else. For that is where
I will find my direction. That is where I will find the answers I need.
That is where I will discover the way You want me to go. So guide
my reading of Your Word today, Lord. Show me what You want me
to see. Tell me what You'd have me memorize and write upon my
heart. Equip me with all I need to know so I can best serve You and
find joy along the way. In Jesus' name, I pray, amen.

STARSTRUCK

The star [the wise men] had seen in the East went before them. It came and stopped over the place where the young Child was. When they saw the star, they were filled with much joy. They went into the house and found the young Child with Mary, His mother. Then they got down before Him and worshiped Him. They opened their bags of riches and gave Him gifts. . . . Then God spoke to them.

MATTHEW 2:9–12 NLV

Jesus, I, like the wise men, followed the light and found You. What joy I discovered in You at our first meeting! What a journey it has been. What wonder I experience each day when I get down on my knees and worship You. I offer You my life, heart, body, mind, and soul. Yet if there are other gifts You would like me to hand over to You or share with others, please show me what they are. For my journey with You has just begun. I want to be Your hands and feet, serving You until I am with You on the other side. Speak to me, Lord. Show me the way to grow ever closer to You. In Your name, I pray, amen.

FRESH START

*Count yourself lucky, how happy you must be—you get a
fresh start, your slate's wiped clean. Count yourself lucky—
God holds nothing against you and you're holding nothing back
from him. When I kept it all inside, my bones turned to powder,
my words became daylong groans. . . . Then I let it all out;
I said, "I'll come clean about my failures to God." Suddenly the
pressure was gone—my guilt dissolved, my sin disappeared.*
PSALM 32:1–3, 5 MSG

Lord, when I keep things from You, when I don't admit to You (or myself) that I've done something wrong, it eats me up inside. One wrongdoing piles up onto another and another and before I know it, I feel like I'm about to implode. So here I am today, Lord, telling You not just the good things I've done but the not-so-good. And I ask Your forgiveness in the process. For then I will once again be able to tap into joy, happy in God, counting myself lucky in the Lord who not only removes my sin and guilt but makes them disappear—forever! What a relief! In Jesus' name, amen.

THE GETAWAY

"Are you tired? Worn out? Burned out on religion? Come to me. Get away with me and you'll recover your life. I'll show you how to take a real rest. Walk with me and work with me—watch how I do it. Learn the unforced rhythms of grace. I won't lay anything heavy or ill-fitting on you. Keep company with me and you'll learn to live freely and lightly."
MATTHEW 11:28–30 MSG

Lord Jesus, joy is elusive at best when I'm not getting the rest I need—spiritually, mentally, emotionally, and physically. I'm worn out, burned out, and just plain tired. Exhausted. So I'm not just coming to You but limping to You. Please take this load of cares, worries, and woes off my back. Help me to give them up, to lay them at Your feet. Show me how to really rest. Teach me how to keep pace with and work with You. Help me to walk in the "unforced rhythms of grace." Teach me how to live this life freely yet more fully. To bear Your light load so I may once more find joy. In Your name, amen.

GROUNDED *in the* WORD

The seed which fell between rocks is like the person who receives the
Word with joy as soon as he hears it. Its root is not deep and it does not
last long. When troubles and suffering come because of the Word, he
gives up and falls away. . . . The seed which fell on good ground is like
the one who hears the Word and understands it. He gives much grain.
MATTHEW 13:20–21, 23 NLV

I am so glad, Lord, that at first hearing, I not only took in Your Word
with joy but let it take root deep within me. But now sometimes on
especially busy days, I find myself not making digging into Your Word
a priority. Help me to change that, Lord. To look to You and Your
Word before my day begins, before my feet hit the floor. Help me to go
deeper and deeper into what You have to say. And help me to grow in
my prayer life. For I want to be one of Your good and faithful servants.
To be so fruitful that I please You more than anyone or anything else,
including myself. Amen.

A HIDING PLACE

Let all who are God-like pray to You while You may be found, because in the floods of much water, they will not touch him. You are my hiding place. You keep me safe from trouble. . . . Many are the sorrows of the sinful. But loving-kindness will be all around the man who trusts in the Lord. Be glad in the Lord and be full of joy, you who are right with God!

PSALM 32:6–7, 10–11 NLV

I am always amazed, Lord, at how You keep me out of troubles seen and unseen. With You next to me, above me, below me, behind me, before me, and within me, I find I am truly safe no matter what comes my way. You, Lord, are my hiding place. To You I run. In You I trust. Surround me not only with Your power, strength, and presence but with all Your unfathomable loving-kindness as I praise You and pray to You. Keep my feet upon Your good path. And in You I will find not only joy but everything I need. In Jesus' name, amen.

GOD-GIVEN JOY

*There is nothing better for a man than to eat and drink and find
joy in his work. I have seen that this also is from the hand of
God. For who can. . .find joy without Him? For God has given
wisdom and much learning and joy to the person who is good in
God's eyes. But to the sinner He has given the work of. . .getting
many riches together to give to the one who pleases God.*
ECCLESIASTES 2:24–26 NLV

Lord, some days I find myself not enjoying anything. But now I realize that's because my thoughts and focus are not on You. For only when I seek You first and bring You to mind throughout my day do I find the joy I crave. So remind me of Your presence, Lord, as I eat and drink. And especially as I work. For I'm not really working for my boss, my family, my church, my spouse, or my school. No, I'm working for You. You are my source of true joy. All I do, I do for You alone. For that work is truly what lasts forever and ever. I pray and praise in Jesus' name, amen.

GRAND PLANS

Sing for joy in the Lord, you who are right with Him. . . .
For the Word of the Lord is right. He is faithful in all He does. . . .
Honor Him. For He spoke, and it was done.
He spoke with strong words, and it stood strong. . . .
The plans of the Lord stand forever. . . .
Happy are the people He has chosen for His own.
PSALM 33:1, 4, 8–9, 11–12 NLV

Your Word is amazing, Father God. Your plans never fail. Your promises are sure and certain. You speak and it is done. You said, "Let there be light," and there was light. Help me, Lord, to trust both You and Your Word. To do as You would have me do. Help me not to be discouraged when things don't go the way I planned. Remind me that *You* are the master planner and that *I can trust* in Your plans. As I abide by Your Word, continually strengthened, guided, and empowered, I find the joy You have waiting for me. For I, Your chosen daughter, rest upon Your promises. Thank You, Father God. Amen.

GIVING CHEERFULLY

He who sows sparingly will also reap sparingly, and he who sows bountifully will also reap bountifully. So let each one give as he purposes in his heart, not grudgingly or of necessity; for God loves a cheerful giver. And God is able to make all grace abound toward you, that you, always having all sufficiency in all things, may have an abundance for every good work.

2 CORINTHIANS 9:6–8 NKJV

When things are difficult financially, Lord, it's hard to give with a cheerful heart. But then I remember Your law: Those who give little will get little, but those who give much will get much. So help me to keep that in mind, knowing that when I give cheerfully, no matter what my circumstances, I will reap cheerfully, beginning with a bountiful crop of joy. And I will also reap contentment. For as I give, You promise to supply me with everything I might need for all the work I'm doing in and for You. Ah, what a relief to live with the knowledge that as I bless others, I can count on You blessing me. Thank You, God, for all this and so much more. Amen.

A FAITHFUL SERVANT

Master, you entrusted to me five talents; see, here I have gained five talents more. His master said to him, Well done, you upright (honorable, admirable) and faithful servant! You have been faithful and trustworthy over a little; I will put you in charge of much. Enter into and share the joy (the delight, the blessedness) which your master enjoys.

MATTHEW 25:20–21 AMPC

I want to be a good servant for You, Lord. I want to use the things with which You have gifted me, not hide them. So, dear Lord, give me the courage I need to step out for You. Help me to nurture the talents You've given me then use them for the good of others and for Your glory. Show me what You would have me do, what You would want me to use to benefit Your kingdom. Help me to be faithful with what You have provided. I long for the day when we meet face-to-face. The day when You open Your arms to me and say, "Well done, My faithful daughter. Come to Me and share the joy and blessings waiting for you." Amen.

A TIME *for* EVERYTHING

For everything there is a season, and a time for every matter
under heaven: a time to be born, and a time to die; a time to plant,
and a time to pluck up what is planted; a time to kill, and a time to
heal; a time to break down, and a time to build up; a time to weep,
and a time to laugh; a time to mourn, and a time to dance.
ECCLESIASTES 3:1–4 ESV

Your Word, Lord, tells me there's a time for everything that happens—life
and death, planting and sowing, weeping and laughing, mourning and
dancing. And that's just the beginning of Your list. But I get it, Lord.
I know some days I'll be sick, praying for Your healing touch. Other
days I may be mourning, seeking Your comfort. But through all these
seasons, Lord, help me to maintain an undercurrent of Your joy, no
matter what my day brings. Help me to realize that someday all these
seasons will pass. In the meantime, I can develop into the woman you
created me to be and dip into Your stream of joy, because I have my
hope in heaven with You. Amen.

HELP and SHIELD

*No king is saved by the power of his strong army. A soldier is
not saved by great strength. A horse cannot be trusted to win a
battle. Its great strength cannot save anyone. . . . Our soul waits
for the Lord. He is our help and our safe cover. For our heart is
full of joy in Him, because we trust in His holy name. O Lord,
let Your loving-kindness be upon us as we put our hope in You.*
PSALM 33:16–17, 20–22 NLV

Lord, sometimes I grow impatient. Instead of waiting for You to move,
I find myself trusting in something *other* than You to save me. I begin to
scheme, to make plans, to search for my own solutions. Yet those ideas
never seem to work, and I just muck things up even more, within and
without. I realize I cannot rely on anyone's strength but Yours, Lord. So
please give me the gift of patience. Help me to wait on You, my help
and shield, knowing that You've got everything under control. Your
timing is the best. As I put my hope in You alone, my heart fills with joy.
For You will work all things out for my good, here and beyond. Amen.

HIDDEN TREASURE

"God's kingdom is like a treasure hidden in a field for years and then accidentally found by a trespasser. The finder is ecstatic— what a find!—and proceeds to sell everything he owns to raise money and buy that field. Or, God's kingdom is like a jewel merchant on the hunt for excellent pearls. Finding one that is flawless, he immediately sells everything and buys it."

MATTHEW 13:44–46 MSG

I know my only path to joy, Lord Jesus, is to sacrifice all that I am and have so that I can gain Your kingdom. Through You, I can reach out to Father God, tap into His power, gain His blessing, get the guidance I need to do as He bids, and so much more. So help me, Jesus, to put You above all things. To seek You before all else. To turn to You upon waking in the morning and then just before I turn out the light at night. For the only joy upon earth is to be focused upon You in heaven. To be in Your presence, feel Your embrace, and be showered by Your love and kindness. What a treasure! What a find! In Your name, I pray and rejoice. Amen.

VALLEY *of* BLESSING

*Jehoshaphat and his people came to take away what they
wanted. . .more than they could carry. . . . It took them three days
to take all the things, because there was so much. They gathered
together in the Valley of Beracah [blessing] on the fourth day. There
they praised and thanked the Lord. . . . They returned to Jerusalem
with joy. For the Lord had filled them with joy by saving them.*

2 CHRONICLES 20:25–27 NLV

How wonderful to know, Lord, that when I'm in trouble and I lay my
problem before You, ask for Your advice, and vow to do as You say, You
move into action. You turn what seem like impossible situations into amazing victories. You turn curses into blessings. When I pray, You do things
beyond my imagining. For there is nothing You cannot do. No problem
You cannot fix. No curse You cannot reverse. And before I know it, I find
myself in the Valley of Blessing. Thank You, Lord, for not just saving me
but championing me. For answering not just one prayer but thousands.
For working in my life and filling me with irrepressible joy in You. Amen.

SEEKING JESUS

Mary Magdalene and the other Mary went to see the tomb. . . . The angel said to the women, "Do not be afraid, for I know that you seek Jesus. . . . He is going before you to Galilee; there you will see him.". . .They departed quickly from the tomb with fear and great joy. . . . And behold, Jesus met them and said, "Greetings!" And they. . .worshiped him.
MATTHEW 28:1, 5, 7–9 ESV

Like the Marys, I too, Lord, am a female disciple. As such, I want to be as faithful to You as they were. Without fear, I look for You. With faith, I find You. And I'm never going to let You go. Be with me now. Teach me to look beyond myself and my assumptions and look to You and Your truth. I want to walk in Your will and way. To hear Your voice speak. To tell others where they can find You, what they can tell You, and how You will appear at the sound of our plea and prayer. Knowing that each day I can and will see You fills me with joy as I bow down at Your feet, ready to worship, to listen, to serve. In Your name, amen.

MY GOD, MY HELP

O send out Your light and Your truth, let them lead me. . .to Your dwelling.
Then will I go to the altar of God, to God, my exceeding joy. . . . Why are
you cast down, O my inner self? And why should you. . .be disquieted
within me? Hope in God and wait expectantly for Him, for I shall yet
praise Him, Who is the help of my [sad] countenance, and my God.
PSALM 43:3–5 AMPC

Lord, I come to Your Word. Send Your light out to me. Allow it to reveal the truth You would have me know. Let the light of Your Word lead me into Your presence, the place where I find my peace, feel Your touch, and experience unfathomable joy. Calm my soul, Lord. Erase my anxiety. Be the balm to my inner self. Renew my hope, Lord. Help me to wait for You, to expect Your goodness to meet my prayer. Give me these moments of quiet. Make my spirit as calm as still water. And as I rest here with You, I give You all my praise and the joy that comes with it. Amen.

A GREAT LIGHT

Gloom will not be upon her who is distressed. . . . The people who walked in darkness have seen a great light. . . . Upon them a light has shined. . . . They rejoice before You. . . . For unto us a Child is born, unto us a Son is given. . . . And His name will be called Wonderful, Counselor, Mighty God, Everlasting Father, Prince of Peace.

ISAIAH 9:1–3, 6 NKJV

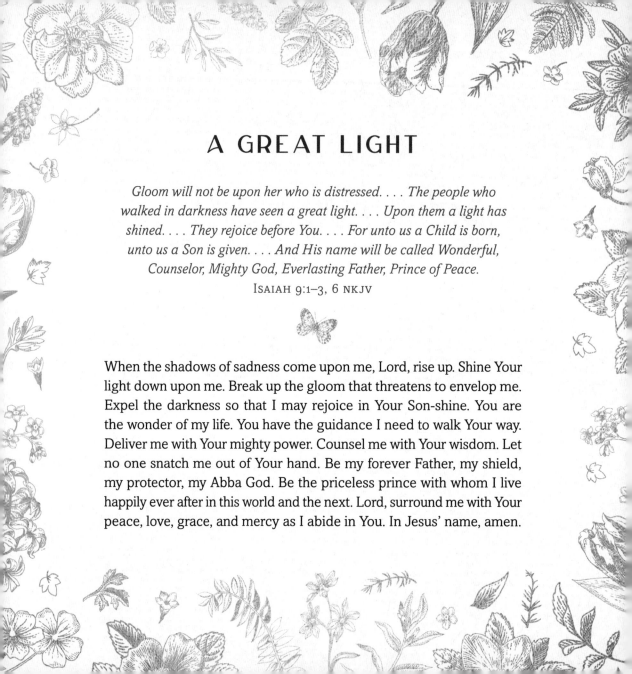

When the shadows of sadness come upon me, Lord, rise up. Shine Your light down upon me. Break up the gloom that threatens to envelop me. Expel the darkness so that I may rejoice in Your Son-shine. You are the wonder of my life. You have the guidance I need to walk Your way. Deliver me with Your mighty power. Counsel me with Your wisdom. Let no one snatch me out of Your hand. Be my forever Father, my shield, my protector, my Abba God. Be the priceless prince with whom I live happily ever after in this world and the next. Lord, surround me with Your peace, love, grace, and mercy as I abide in You. In Jesus' name, amen.

EYE OPENER

They began to recognize God and praise and give thanks. . . . God has visited His people [in order to help and care for and provide for them]! And this report concerning [Jesus] spread. . . . In that very hour Jesus was healing many [people] of sicknesses and distressing bodily plagues and evil spirits, and to many who were blind He gave [a free, gracious, joy-giving gift of] sight.
LUKE 7:16–17, 21 AMPC

I am still amazed, Father God, by the gift You have given me in Your Son, Jesus. Through Him, You came and walked among us. You are and have been my helper, caretaker, and provider. You heal me from the sickness within my body, mind, spirit, and soul. You de-stress me, taking away my cares, woes, anxieties, and issues. You have opened my eyes to the truth of Your Word. Through that lens, I see the path You want me to take, the road You want me to travel. Thank You for the joy-giving gift of Jesus, the one who continually opens my eyes, mind, and heart so that I can see You. In His name, I pray, amen.

GOOD WORDS

Lying is in the heart of those who plan what is bad, but those who plan peace have joy. . . . The Lord hates lying lips, but those who speak the truth are His joy. . . . Worry in the heart of a man weighs it down, but a good word makes it glad. . . . Life is in the way of those who are right with God, and in its path there is no death.
PROVERBS 12:20, 22, 25, 28 NLV

You, Lord, are the master of truth and the archenemy of the father of lies. So, Lord, help me to be very aware of all the words I allow to leave my lips. Keep me on the path of truth so that I will be a person who makes plans for peace. For I want to please You and partake of all the joy that offers. I realize worries are nothing more than lies I tell myself. They imply that I don't trust You. So filter my words, Lord. Keep any and all untruths from my mind and lips because my desire is to be right with You in thought, word, and deed. Amen.

GOOD NEWS

*There were shepherds in the fields. . .watching their flocks of sheep
at night. The angel of the Lord came to them. The shining-greatness
of the Lord shone around them. They were very much afraid. The
angel said to them, "Do not be afraid. See! I bring you good news
of great joy which is for all people. Today, One Who saves from the
punishment of sin has been born. . . . He is Christ the Lord."*
LUKE 2:8–11 NLV

I love how You gave Your Son's birth announcement to humankind,
Lord. You directed angels to proclaim the great news, the Good News,
about Jesus to a simple band of shepherds, socially considered one
of the lowest groups of people. The angel's first words to them were,
"Don't be afraid. I've got some good news that's going to bring you great
happiness. Jesus, God's Son, will save you!" When *I* first heard Your
news, it seemed too good to be true—that someone sacrificed all so
that I could live for You, see You, pray to You. Yet that good news was,
still is, and forever will be true. Thank You for the joy I find in Jesus,
Your Son and my Lord, King, and Savior. Amen.

THE VOICE *of* JOY

Show your happiness, all peoples! Call out to God with the voice of joy! For the Lord Most High is to be feared. He is a great King over all the earth. He sets people under us, and nations under our feet. He chooses for us what is to be ours, the pride of Jacob, whom He loves. . . . God rules over the nations. God sits on His holy throne.

PSALM 47:1–4, 8 NLV

It seems so easy, Lord, for me to get weighed down by world news. I sometimes feel so helpless, unable to stop the tide of evil. Yet that's not how You would have me be. For I'm Your child. You're my King, the one who rules over all things, who chooses what I am to be and have in this life. You want me to be filled with joy. For what kind of witness would I be for You if I were constantly worried, frightened, upset, and anxious? So, Lord, today, right here, right now, turn my frown upside down! Give me that deep sense of joy from which I can draw—no matter what's happening within and without. In Jesus' name, I pray and praise, amen.

THE HABIT *of* JOYFUL HOPE

Let us. . .rejoice in our sufferings, knowing that pressure and affliction
and hardship produce patient and unswerving endurance. And
endurance (fortitude) develops maturity of character (approved faith
and tried integrity). And character [of this sort] produces [the habit
of] joyful and confident hope of eternal salvation. Such hope never
disappoints or deludes or shames us, for God's love has been poured
out in our hearts through the Holy Spirit Who has been given to us.
ROMANS 5:3–5 AMPC

Even when I feel as if I'm going through the wringer, Lord, I have hope.
For Your Word tells me that my troubles are actually good for me. They
strengthen me. They bring me back to You. They remind me of the joy I
have because I know I will one day be with You in heaven forever. And
it is that hope that keeps me going, looking to You, feeling Your love
bloom within me through the Holy Spirit You've given me. Within You,
Lord, I have all I need not just to get through this life but to experience
Your abundant peace and provision amid the process. Amen.

A FOREVER GUIDE

Fair and beautiful in elevation, is the joy of all the earth—Mount Zion
[the City of David]. . . . God has made Himself known in her palaces
as a Refuge (a High Tower and a Stronghold). . . . We have thought of
Your steadfast love, O God, in the midst of Your temple. . . . For this God
is our God forever and ever; He will be our guide [even] until death.
PSALM 48:2–3, 9, 14 AMPC

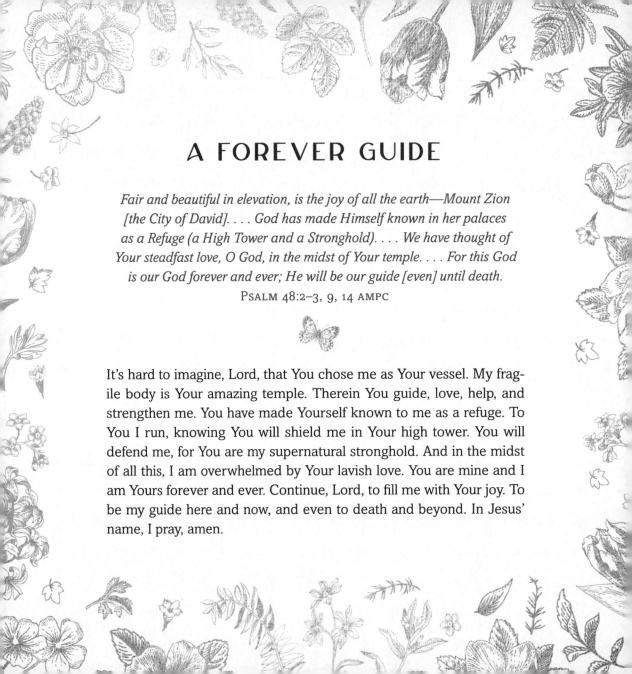

It's hard to imagine, Lord, that You chose me as Your vessel. My fragile body is Your amazing temple. Therein You guide, love, help, and strengthen me. You have made Yourself known to me as a refuge. To You I run, knowing You will shield me in Your high tower. You will defend me, for You are my supernatural stronghold. And in the midst of all this, I am overwhelmed by Your lavish love. You are mine and I am Yours forever and ever. Continue, Lord, to fill me with Your joy. To be my guide here and now, and even to death and beyond. In Jesus' name, I pray, amen.

OCCUPIED *with* JOY

What I have seen to be good and fitting is to eat and drink and
find enjoyment in all the toil with which one toils under the sun
the few days of his life that God has given him, for this is his lot.
Everyone also to whom God has given wealth and possessions and
power to enjoy them, and to accept his lot and rejoice in his toil—
this is the gift of God. For he will not much remember the days of
his life because God keeps him occupied with joy in his heart.

ECCLESIASTES 5:18–20 ESV

This is what I want, Lord. To enjoy the life You have given me. To enjoy
whatever I eat and drink and whatever work I put my hand to. For this
is the life with which You have so wonderfully blessed me. I want to be
so focused on all the good things in my life, so content with what You
have gifted me, that I don't get hung up on the negative things. I don't
want to allow the world's woes to put a shadow upon my blessings from
You. Keep me occupied, Lord, with all the joy You have already planted
in my heart, today and every day. Amen.

THE AGENDA *for* REJOICING

Jesus said. . ."See what I've given you? Safe passage as you walk on snakes and scorpions, and protection from every assault of the Enemy. No one can put a hand on you. All the same, the great triumph is not in your authority over evil, but in God's authority over you and presence with you. Not what you do for God but what God does for you—that's the agenda for rejoicing."

LUKE 10:19–20 MSG

You have provided me with so many blessings, Jesus, it's hard to count them all. You give me safe passage through this life. Because I live in You, nothing can ever really touch me. No power can ever get through because You're busy protecting me. In fact, no one can even take me out of Your hand! But that's not where my real triumph is. My real triumph is Abba God's power over me and His presence within me. It's not about what I do for God, how He works through me. No. My real cause for rejoicing is all about what He does for me! Thank You, Jesus, for all the blessings You so readily give me and all the ways You work in my life. Amen.

OPEN MINDS

At that, Jesus rejoiced, exuberant in the Holy Spirit. "I thank you, Father, Master of heaven and earth, that you hid these things from the know-it-alls and showed them to these innocent newcomers. Yes, Father, it pleased you to do it this way." . . . He then turned in a private aside to his disciples. "Fortunate the eyes that see what you're seeing. . .to hear what you are hearing."
LUKE 10:21, 23 MSG

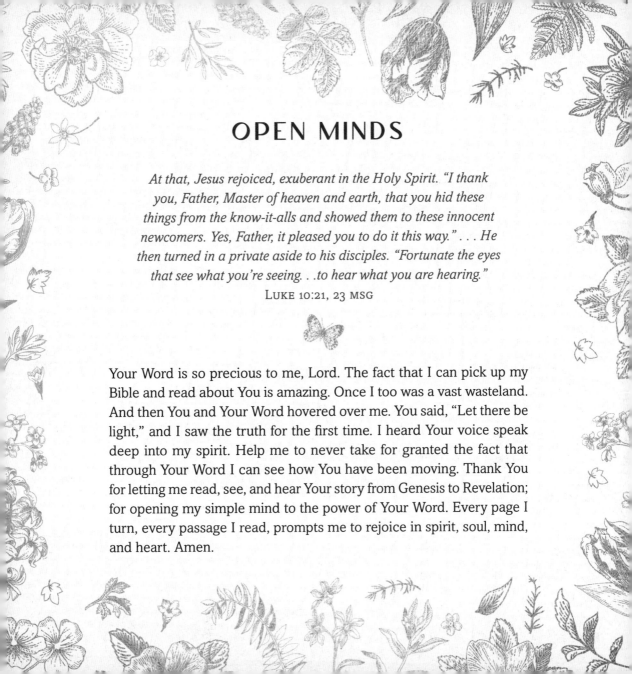

Your Word is so precious to me, Lord. The fact that I can pick up my Bible and read about You is amazing. Once I too was a vast wasteland. And then You and Your Word hovered over me. You said, "Let there be light," and I saw the truth for the first time. I heard Your voice speak deep into my spirit. Help me to never take for granted the fact that through Your Word I can see how You have been moving. Thank You for letting me read, see, and hear Your story from Genesis to Revelation; for opening my simple mind to the power of Your Word. Every page I turn, every passage I read, prompts me to rejoice in spirit, soul, mind, and heart. Amen.

LOST *and* FOUND

"What woman, having ten silver coins, if she loses one coin, does not light a lamp, sweep the house, and search carefully until she finds it? And when she has found it, she calls her friends and neighbors together, saying, 'Rejoice with me, for I have found the piece which I lost!' Likewise, I say to you, there is joy in the presence of the angels of God over one sinner who repents."

LUKE 15:8–10 NKJV

Lord, through Your Word I realize I can, with Your help, bring joy not only to others but to You and Your angels. I know there are many people out there, many sheep who have yet to find You, the good shepherd. Yet I also know that You can use me to find them. To be the light that attracts them to You. So help me, Lord, to be that light. To allow Your love and joy to shine through me so powerfully that others will want what I have—You. To that end, I pray, Lord, that Your Holy Spirit would lead the way. That He would use me to turn nonbelievers to You. And that Your angels would then share in the joy of a lost sheep found. In Jesus' name, amen.

A QUENCHED THIRST

O God, You are my God. I will look for You with all my heart and strength. My soul is thirsty for You. My flesh is weak wanting You in a dry and tired land where there is no water. . . . I have seen Your power and Your shining-greatness. . . . I will lift up my hands in Your name. My soul will be filled. . . . And my mouth praises You with lips of joy.

PSALM 63:1–2, 4–5 NLV

Oh Lord, my God, I need You. I need Your presence, Your cooling shade, Your warming arms. You are everything I desire and thirst for. I am desperate for Your comfort and love. Give me some good news through Your Word. Show me Your power and might. Imbue me with Your love and grace. Draw me out of myself and into Your presence. For here alone do I find my source, my provision, my strength, my refuge. In You I am home. In You I have hope. I'm lifting up my hands, Lord, to praise and worship You. Fill my soul with Your Spirit. And my mouth will respond with praises of joy. In Jesus' name, amen.

MOVED *with* COMPASSION

When he came to himself, he said. . .I will get up and go to my father,
and I will say to him, Father, I have sinned. . . . While he was still a long
way off, his father saw him and was moved with pity and tenderness
[for him]; and he ran and embraced him and kissed him [fervently]. . . .
The father said. . .Let us revel and feast and be happy and make merry.
LUKE 15:17–18, 20, 22–23 AMPC

Sometimes, Lord, I don't realize how far I have strayed from You. But then when I come to myself, I know what I have to say. I have to tell You, in my own words, how I have erred and made a misstep. Help me right here and now to ask for Your forgiveness. Help me to picture You as a Father who is looking for me, waiting for me, even when I'm still a long way off. Let me see You as a Father who is moved with love and compassion for me. Open Your arms, Lord, as I turn this corner and run into Your embrace. Grant me Your forgiveness. And may we end this moment by reveling in each other's company, full of joy, feasting on our mutual love. Amen.

AT HOME *in* GOD

*Silence is praise to you, Zion-dwelling God, and also obedience. You
hear the prayer in it all. We all arrive at your doorstep sooner or later,
loaded with guilt, our sins too much for us—but you get rid of them once
and for all. Blessed are the chosen! Blessed the guest at home in your
place! We expect our fill of good things in your house, your heavenly
manse. . . . Dawn and dusk take turns calling, "Come and worship."*
PSALM 65:1–4, 8 MSG

In the stillness of this moment, Lord, I come before You in silent wonder
of who You are, what You have done, and how You have worked in my
life. Hear my prayer, Lord, as my lips praise You. Free me of the missteps,
the mistakes I have made, the guilt that weighs me down. Lord, cleanse
me of all shadows. Leave only Your light behind and within me. Here, in
Your presence, I feel I am home. Thank You for opening Your door to
me. For choosing me, saving me, and loving me. What joy I find within
Your heavenly dwelling, my provider, my God. Here I find all I need.
Here, at Your feet, I worship. In Jesus' name, amen.

SEEKERS

Zacchaeus. . .was a chief tax collector and was rich. And he was seeking to see who Jesus was, but on account of the crowd he could not. . . . So he ran on ahead and climbed up into a sycamore tree to see him. . . . When Jesus came to the place, he looked up and said to him, "Zacchaeus, hurry and come down, for I must stay at your house today." So he hurried and came down and received him joyfully.

LUKE 19:2–6 ESV

Rich or poor, large or small, Lord, may I always run to catch sight of You. May I not let crowds or distance dissuade me from finding You. You, Lord Jesus, know all who seek Your face. You know our names, stories, conditions. And still You call us to Yourself, telling us to speedily welcome You into our homes, our hearts. And all who do, all who truly want to see Your face, just as they are, Lord, those are the ones with whom You spend time. Those are the ones You save. Those are the ones who revel in the joy of Your presence. Speak to me, Lord. Just as I am. In You, I pray, amen.

WHITER THAN SNOW

O God, favor me because of Your lovingkindness. Take away my
wrong-doing because of the greatness of Your loving-pity. . . . I have
sinned against You, and You only. . . . Take away my sin, and I
will be clean. Wash me, and I will be whiter than snow. Make me
hear joy and happiness. . . . Make a clean heart in me, O God.
PSALM 51:1, 4, 7–8, 10 NLV

Lord, I have hurt someone. I have injured another person. And I'm filled
with remorse. For not only have I harmed another, but I have disobeyed
You in the process. Thus I have sinned against You at the same time.
Both sins bring me shame, Lord. But doing wrong to You truly hurts
my heart. So I come to You upon my knees. I ask You for forgiveness.
For cleansing. For a new heart and a fresh start. Wash me within and
without, Lord. Supply me with the words of apology to the person I
have harmed. At the same time, Lord, help me to forgive those who
have hurt me. And before I leave this prayer, this place, this space, Lord,
"make me hear joy and happiness" in You once more. Amen.

GRAND OPENINGS

*They said to Him, "Stay with us. . . ." As [Jesus] sat at the table
with them, He took the bread and gave thanks and broke it.
Then He gave it to them.And their eyes were opened and they
knew Him. Then He left them and could not be seen. They
said to each other, "Were not our hearts filled with joy when He
talked to us on the road about what the Holy Writings said?"*

LUKE 24:29–32 NLV

As I walk upon the road of life, Lord, thinking about what I've seen
and heard, walk with me. Stay with me. Reveal to me the meaning
of Your Word. Open up my mind as I read Your scriptures. Open
my eyes so that I can see You in all things, all events, from Genesis
to Revelation and beyond. Feed me the bread of Your Word. Break
it open for me so that its wisdom can pour out. Talk to me through
every letter, line, verse, and chapter. Fill my heart with the joy of
Your Word as we walk and talk on this road and beyond. In Your
name, I pray, live, move, and have my being, amen.

NIGHT HOURS

*My lips will praise You because Your loving-kindness is better than
life. . . . On my bed I remember You. I think of You through the
hours of the night. For You have been my help. And I sing for joy
in the shadow of Your wings. My soul holds on to You. Your right
hand holds me up. . . . All who are faithful to God will be full of joy.*
PSALM 63:3, 6–8, 11 NLV

Lord, there is no better or greater thing in my life than Your love for me
and Your never-ending kindness to me. When I climb into bed at the
end of the day, I think of You. I pray to You. I ask You for blessings, for
compassion on me and those I love. And amid that nightly prayer to
You, I not only fall asleep but fall into Your arms. Thank You for holding
me, helping me, hiding me, and hovering over me. In You I find my rest,
my shelter, my peace. I'm clinging to You, Lord, holding on tight. For
You are my salvation. You are my joy. In You alone do I trust and find
my way. Amen.

WONDER and JOY

"Why are you troubled, and why do doubts arise in your hearts?
See my hands and my feet, that it is I myself. Touch me, and
see. For a spirit does not have flesh and bones as you see that
I have." And when he had said this, he showed them his hands
and his feet. And while they still disbelieved for joy and were
marveling, he said to them, "Have you anything here to eat?"
LUKE 24:38–41 ESV

You amaze me, Lord. You show up, out of nowhere, whenever I need You. You tell me to calm down. Not to worry. Not to allow thoughts of doubt into my heart or mind. You point me to You, revealing all that You are and ever have been. You tell me the truth. That You are the Son of God, the one who died to save my soul. The one raised from the dead who lives to bring me to Father God. Some days, Lord, I cannot believe what You have done for me. I sit back amazed yet full of joy. Then You help me to get on with the needs of the day, continually providing for me, leading me, guiding me. Oh Lord, You are my wonder and joy. Amen.

A WILLING SPIRIT

*Make a clean heart in me, O God. Give me a new spirit that will
not be moved. Do not throw me away from where You are. And do
not take Your Holy Spirit from me. Let the joy of Your saving power
return to me. And give me a willing spirit to obey you. . . . Then my
tongue will sing with joy about how right and good You are.*
PSALM 51:10–12, 14 NLV

I've fallen short, Lord. I've misstepped. And so here I am before You,
asking for forgiveness. For my sins to be washed away. For a clean
heart—and a new spirit. One that will be stronger, not so easily led
into sin, not so easily lured into temptation. Draw me near to You,
Lord. I want to snuggle up close, to feel Your breath, to join my spirit
with Yours. Return to me the joy of Your saving power. And make my
spirit willingly obey You. For I know my true joy and path lie in Your
way, not my own. Set me straight, Lord. Prepare me and my path as I
joyfully praise You. Amen.

OPEN *to* UNDERSTANDING

He went on to open their understanding of the Word of God, showing them how to read their Bibles. . . . He then led them out of the city over to Bethany. Raising his hands he blessed them, and while blessing them, made his exit, being carried up to heaven. And they were on their knees, worshiping him. They returned to Jerusalem bursting with joy. They spent all their time in the Temple praising God.
LUKE 24:45, 50–52 MSG

I need Your help, Lord. I need You to open my mind, heart, and eyes as I read the Word. I want to understand what You're writing, saying, teaching. I want to love what You want me to love. I want to see the words You want me to see. I want to think the thoughts You want me to think. So lead me, Lord. Bless me as I lift my hands in praise and fall on my knees in worship. Give me such a good understanding of You and Your ways that I may return to and approach this earthly world bursting with joy as I praise and pray in Your name. Amen.

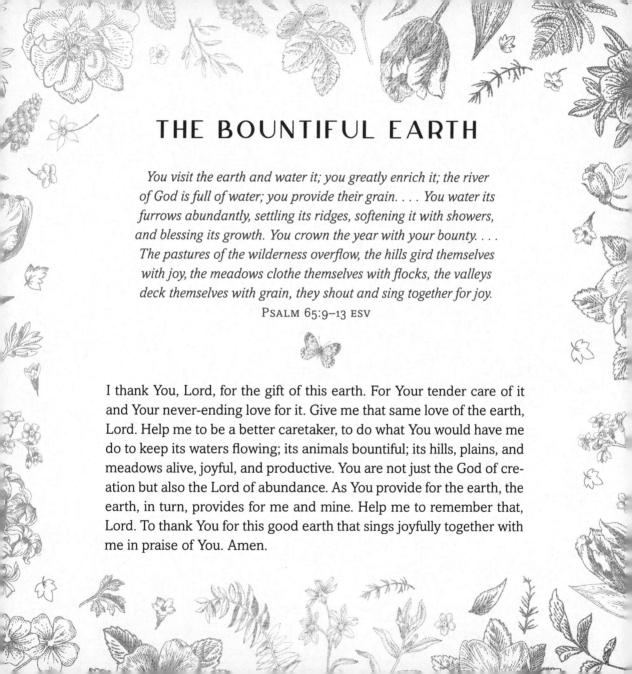

THE BOUNTIFUL EARTH

You visit the earth and water it; you greatly enrich it; the river of God is full of water; you provide their grain. . . . You water its furrows abundantly, settling its ridges, softening it with showers, and blessing its growth. You crown the year with your bounty. . . . The pastures of the wilderness overflow, the hills gird themselves with joy, the meadows clothe themselves with flocks, the valleys deck themselves with grain, they shout and sing together for joy.

PSALM 65:9–13 ESV

I thank You, Lord, for the gift of this earth. For Your tender care of it and Your never-ending love for it. Give me that same love of the earth, Lord. Help me to be a better caretaker, to do what You would have me do to keep its waters flowing; its animals bountiful; its hills, plains, and meadows alive, joyful, and productive. You are not just the God of creation but also the Lord of abundance. As You provide for the earth, the earth, in turn, provides for me and mine. Help me to remember that, Lord. To thank You for this good earth that sings joyfully together with me in praise of You. Amen.

GENUINE JOY

Unlike the culture around you, always dragging you down to its level of immaturity, God brings the best out of you, develops well-formed maturity in you. . . . If you're called to give aid to people in distress, keep your eyes open and be quick to respond; if you work with the disadvantaged, don't let yourself get irritated with them or depressed by them. Keep a smile on your face. Love from the center of who you are; don't fake it.
ROMANS 12:2, 8–9 MSG

Help me, Lord Jesus, to be different from the culture around me. Lift me up to You, lest I be dragged down into the chaos of this world. Bring out the best in me so that I can be a useful part of Your body. Open my eyes to people whom You want me to help. Give me the resources to lift them as You have lifted me. Keep me from getting irritated by those who are weak, suffering, disadvantaged, poor, or depressed. Help me to keep my mind, heart, and ears open. Make me a good listener, free of judgment. And above all, give me such deep joy that no matter who I am helping, my smile toward them is genuine, an offshoot of my happiness in and with You. Amen.

PRESENT JOY

[The once-exiled and now returned Israelites] sang, praising and giving thanks to the Lord, saying, "For He is good, for His loving-kindness is upon Israel forever." All the people called out with a loud voice when they praised the Lord because the work on the house of the Lord had begun. But many. . .had seen the first house of the Lord. And they cried with a loud voice. . . . But many called out for joy in a loud voice.
 EZRA 3:11–12 NLV

Sometimes, Lord, I can really mess up a good thing. Then when I try to rebuild, the new doesn't seem like it will be better than—or even as good as—what was there before. In either case, Lord, help me to have hope. To rejoice at whatever new thing You are doing. Although it may be okay to spend a little time grieving over the loss of what once was, don't let me stay there. Give me the courage to look away from the past and into the present. Help me to praise what You are doing now. To see the new thing You have prepared. To remember how good You have been, are now, and always will be. Enwrap me in Your present joy. In Jesus' name, amen.

THE TRUE SOURCE

"You heard the words that I said, 'I am not the Christ, but I have been sent before Him.' The man who has just been married has the bride. The friend of the man just married stands at his side and listens to him. He has joy when he hears the voice of the man just married. I am full of this joy. He must become more important. I must become less important."

JOHN 3:28–30 NLV

Jesus, nothing gives me more joy than when I bring You to the attention of a nonbeliever—and then that nonbeliever begins to experience You, follow You, love and worship You as I do. But afterward, Lord, help me to slip away to the sidelines. To get out of the way of Your light. Help me to be humble enough to let the newly born in You know *You* are the source of our joy. That You are the true path, the real way, and I am just a signpost along the road. For You alone are the one and only Son. The one who plants and nourishes the joy in our lives and love in our hearts. In Your name, I pray, amen.

VOICES RAISED *in* PRAISE

Raise the voice of joy to God. . . . Come and see what God has done. . . . He changed the sea into dry land. They passed through the river on foot. There we were full of joy in Him. . . . We went through fire and through water. But You brought us out into a place where we have much more than we need. . . . Honor and thanks be to God!
PSALM 66:1, 5–6, 12, 20 NLV

I may sometimes go through some rough patches, Lord, but somehow You always get me out. You make a way where there seems to be no way. You do the impossible when I'm between a rock and a hard place. You rescue me in a way that is so far beyond what I ever could have dreamed or imagined. And somehow in the process, I end up better off than I was before! So I'm raising my voice of joy to You, Lord. Thank You for all You have done and continue to do in my life. All my love, honor, and thanks go to You. In Jesus' name, I praise, amen.

HAPPY *in* HOPE

Hold on to whatever is good. Love each other. . . . Show respect for each other. . . . Work for the Lord with a heart full of love for Him. Be happy in your hope. Do not give up when trouble comes. Do not let anything stop you from praying. Share what you have with Christian brothers who are in need. Give meals and a place to stay to those who need it.

ROMANS 12:9–13 NLV

Lord, I want to become the woman You designed me to be. One of the spirit and not the flesh. So I'm going to focus on all things good. I'm going to love and respect whomever I meet. I'm going to work for You with all my heart. And I'll be ecstatically happy because I have hope—in You, Your kingdom, Your promises, Your precepts, and Your Word. Such hope will keep me joyful and spiritually alive— even in the midst of trouble. For I'll know You are with me—now and forever. And as I walk Your way, I'll find myself just where You want me: happily serving those in need, knowing that as I do so, I'm really serving You. In Jesus' name, amen.

OPEN WIDE

*Sing aloud to God our Strength! Shout for joy. . . .You called in distress and
I delivered you; I answered you in the secret place of thunder; I tested you
at the waters of Meribah. . . . I am the Lord your God, Who brought you
up out of the land of Egypt. Open your mouth wide and I will fill it. . . .
Oh, that My people would listen to Me, that Israel would walk in My ways!*
PSALM 81:1, 7, 10, 13 AMPC

From You, Lord, I get the strength to overcome. To You, I shout for joy.
Because whenever I call, Lord, You answer. When I am in need, You
respond. You are the one who continually rescues me. You part the sea
so I can flee from my foes. You subdue rulers so I can find my way to
freedom in You. When I am hungry, You fill my mouth with food. When
I am thirsty, You provide water from a rock. My joy lies in following You,
obeying You, listening to You. For only when I walk in Your way am I
on the right road, to joy and to Your kingdom. Amen.

A SPECIAL PLACE

Do not let your hearts be troubled (distressed, agitated). You believe in and adhere to and trust in and rely on God; believe in and adhere to and trust in and rely also on Me. In My Father's house there are many dwelling places (homes). If it were not so, I would have told you; for I am going away to prepare a place for you. . . . Where I am going, you know the way.

JOHN 14:1–2, 4 AMPC

Some days the woes, worries, and what-ifs come tumbling upon me, Lord. I get weighted down by this world so easily. And then I remember Your words. You've told me not to let my heart and mind be troubled but to trust in You, to lean on and rely on God. You've made it clear that You have a place for me in Father God's house. A room that You have prepared—just for me! I know the way there, so I'm running to You, Lord. Lift me up to that room, the one where I'll find You. That secret place of joy, where all my troubles fade away as I melt into You. Amen.

FROM SORROW *to* SOLUTION

The king said to me, Why do you look sad. . . ? This is nothing but
sorrow of heart. Then I was very much afraid. . . . The king said to
me, For what do you ask? So I prayed to the God of heaven. And I
said to [him]. . .I ask that you will send me to Judah. . . . And the king
granted what I asked, for the good hand of my God was upon me.
NEHEMIAH 2:2, 4–5, 8 AMPC

When I am sad, Lord, when my heart is filled with sorrow, give me
courage and allay my fears. Give me the words to speak to You so that I
can get out from under my cloud of emotions and into the light of Your
truth. Prompt me to pray, to lay out my concerns and worries before
You. Help me to seek Your will. Whether my prayer be long or short,
spoken or silent, hear my words. Tell me what You would have me say
or do. Show me which direction to go. For in You alone do I find the
path to take, the courage and joy to go forward, walking with Your good
hand upon me. Amen.

NEVER ALONE

*"The Father. . .will give you another Helper, to be with you
forever. . . . I will not leave you as orphans; I will come to you. . . .
If anyone loves me, he will keep my word, and my Father will
love him, and we will come to him and make our home with him. . . .
Peace I leave with you. . . . Let not your hearts be troubled."*
JOHN 14:16, 18, 23, 27 ESV

There are times, Jesus, when I feel all alone. When it seems as if everyone has deserted me. I reach out, but no one is there—except for You. Thank You for promising never to leave me. For coming when I call You. For providing me with Your Spirit, the helper who takes my moans and groans and translates them into a prayer for God's ear. Because I love You and keep Your Word, You and the Spirit have made a home within me. What peace I find in You. What joy it gives my heart to know You will always be here with me. In Your name, I pray and praise, amen.

HOW BEAUTIFUL

How beautiful are the places where You live, O Lord of all! My soul wants and even becomes weak from wanting to be in the house of the Lord. My heart and my flesh sing for joy to the living God. Even the bird has found a home. The swallow has found a nest for herself where she may lay her young at Your altars, O Lord of all, my King and my God.

PSALM 84:1–3 NLV

Where You live, Lord, must be amazing. I cannot even wrap my mind around what it might look like. Greater than the Taj Mahal. More amazing than the Grand Canyon. More beautiful than a Caribbean island. Wherever You are, in heaven or on earth, my soul longs to meet You, to be with You. There's no place I desire to be more than where You are. For You accept the humblest and simplest of creatures. When I, Your daughter, come to You, I feel like a princess in a palace. For in You, my Father and King, is where I find my real home. Where love, warmth, joy, and wonder rise up to greet me. As I follow Your light, I enter in, oh Lord, and bow at Your throne. Amen.

JOY RUNNING OVER

I am the Vine and you are the branches. Get your life from Me. Then
I will live in you and you will give much fruit. You can do nothing
without Me. . . . If you get your life from Me and My Words live in
you, ask whatever you want. It will be done for you. . . . I have told
you these things so My joy may be in you and your joy may be full.
JOHN 15:5, 7, 11 NLV

You, Jesus, are so precious. It's in You that I find my source of love, light, and life. For I can do nothing—and *am* nothing—without You. You feed me, nourish me, and give me the power to follow Your commandments. To love the Father with all my heart, mind, soul, and strength. And to love others as I love myself. Help me, Lord, to live my life *in* You, to obey Your teachings. For when I do, You will not only live in *me* but will grant me whatever I ask. Thank You for the joy this brings—Yours in me, and mine running over! In Your name, I pray, amen.

PEACE-FILLED LIVING

Pray and give thanks for those who make trouble for you. Yes, pray for them instead of talking against them. Be happy with those who are happy. Be sad with those who are sad. Live in peace with each other. Do not act or think with pride. Be happy to be with poor people. Keep yourself from thinking you are so wise. . . . As much as you can, live in peace with all men.
ROMANS 12:14–16, 18 NLV

The people of this world have become so contentious, Lord. It seems to be a battleground of continuous disagreements. And I know this is not Your way, for spiteful comebacks suck the joy and peace right out of life. Lord, I want to take the higher road. So give me the words to pray for those who make trouble for me. Help me not to say anything bad against them but to thank You for bringing them into my life. Help me to treat others with compassion and to be the peacemaker in all situations. In other words, Lord Jesus, give me the strength, courage, and fortitude to be more like You—acquainted with sorrow yet, in praying and serving others, transformed by joy. In Your name, I pray, amen.

BIRTHING JOY

*When a woman gives birth, she has a hard time, there's no
getting around it. But when the baby is born, there is joy in
the birth. This new life in the world wipes out memory of the
pain. The sadness you have right now is similar to that pain,
but the coming joy is also similar. When I see you again, you'll
be full of joy, and it will be a joy no one can rob from you.*
JOHN 16:21–23 MSG

It's so true, Lord! When a woman is pregnant, she and her body go
through a lot. First she's happy she's going to have a baby. Then
she may have morning sickness, become physically awkward, and
have to get up several times at night to relieve herself. And that's
just the prelude to the overture of pain that comes with giving birth.
Yet when she holds that baby, that gift of life in her arms, the love
she has for that child erases all the prior pain. And it's the same
with lots of other things in life, Lord. I may have hard times, but
because You're with me through the trials, I know I'll find the joy I
desire in You, from pain to pleasure, from beginning to end. Amen.

HAPPY *in* JESUS

O Lord God of all, hear my prayer. . . . Look upon our safe-covering,
O God. And look upon the face of Your chosen one. For a day in Your
house is better than a thousand outside. . . . For the Lord God is a sun and
a safe-covering. . . . He holds back nothing good from those who walk in the
way that is right. O Lord of all, how happy is the man who trusts in You!
PSALM 84:8–12 NLV

After a week in the world, Lord, I run to Your house of worship. I run to join Your other children in prayer and praise as we lift our eyes and hearts to You. Thank You, Lord, for keeping me safe, looking out for me from Monday to Saturday. Thank You for coming into our presence when we come to Your house. Every minute there is so precious. For I see Your love and light in those who worship with me, Lord. We happily trust You, Lord, to help us, to meet with us, to keep us strong as we endeavor to serve You. Amen.

GENTLE STRENGTH

*How happy are those who live in Your house! They are always
giving thanks to You. How happy is the man whose strength
is in You and in whose heart are the roads to Zion! As they pass
through the dry valley of Baca, they make it a place of good
water. The early rain fills the pools with good also. They go from
strength to strength. Every one of them stands before God.*
PSALM 84:4–7 NLV

The more time I spend with You, Jesus—studying Your Word, praying
Your way, absorbing Your truths, following Your will—the stronger I seem
to become. At each point, in each trial, I learn more, grow more, and
find myself closer and closer to You. Yet at the same time my strength
is increasing, the gentler I become and the more I find peace, even in
the midst of trial. All this gives me such joy. The unshakable kind. The
joy that makes my foundation in You so firm. Thank You, Lord, for being
there—everywhere I look. Everywhere I love. Everywhere I roam, from
strength to strength, I'm home in You. Amen.

COMPLETED *with* JOY

Forget about deciding what's right for each other. . . . God's kingdom isn't a matter of what you put in your stomach, for goodness' sake. It's what God does with your life as he sets it right, puts it together, and completes it with joy. Your task is to single-mindedly serve Christ. Do that and you'll kill two birds with one stone: pleasing the God above you and proving your worth to the people around you.

ROMANS 14:13, 17–18 MSG

Jesus, there are so many traditions, rules, and methods people say should be used to serve You, love You, pray to You, worship You, and more. It's mind-boggling. All I want is to follow what You would have me do. So help me to focus on You more than any other thing. Help me to dive deeply into Your Word for direction. To concentrate on serving You and You alone. For I know when I do, the Father will use me as He desires and fill my life with joy. What more can a woman ask but to please Father God and be of worth to those around her? In Jesus' name, amen.

LORD KNOWS

The heart knows its own bitterness, and no stranger shares its joy. . . . In the reverent and worshipful fear of the Lord there is strong confidence, and His children shall always have a place of refuge. . . . A calm and undisturbed mind and heart are the life and health of the body. . . . Wisdom rests [silently] in the mind and heart of him who has understanding.

PROVERBS 14:10, 26, 30, 33 AMPC

Only You can fully understand and empathize with the sorrow I bear in my heart, Lord. And yet at the same time, only You can fully understand, know, and take part in the joy I experience as well. Whether joyful or sad, I know You are with me, tending me, caring for me, crying or laughing with me. In You I find shelter from the storms of life. You give me the peace I crave. You calm my heart, quiet my spirit. Give me the wisdom, Lord, to run to You whether I am in tears or rolling with laughter. Share my life, sorrows, and joys, Lord, as I live and move in You. Amen.

WALKING on AIR

Blessed are the people who know the passwords of praise, who shout on parade in the bright presence of God. Delighted, they dance all day long; they know who you are, what you do—they can't keep it quiet! Your vibrant beauty has gotten inside us— you've been so good to us! We're walking on air! All we are and have we owe to God, Holy God of Israel, our King!
PSALM 89:15–18 MSG

At times, Lord, I can't see the forest for the trees; I can't see the good within the bad. Although that seems the natural way of humankind, I know that's not how You want us to view the world. For when we see only the perils and darkness, we miss the safety and light. So help change me up, Lord. Help me to focus more on the showers of blessings, the good, the light. Prompt me to dance and shout in praise. Remind me of who You are, what You've done. Fill me with such joy and delight that I'm lifted way above the earth, praising You all the day. In Jesus' name, I pray, amen.

FROM SADNESS *to* GLADNESS

"You're going to be in deep mourning while the godless world throws a party. You'll be sad, very sad, but your sadness will develop into gladness. . . . This is what I want you to do: Ask the Father for whatever is in keeping with the things I've revealed to you. Ask in my name, according to my will, and he'll most certainly give it to you. Your joy will be a river overflowing its banks!"

JOHN 16:20, 23–24 MSG

I'm looking to You for direction, Jesus. I want to walk in Your way, according to Your will. You are the way and truth and life. While You were here on earth and now while You're in heaven, You know exactly what's going to happen in my life and why. You have said my path lies in You. Show me, Jesus, what You would have me pray for, what You would have me ask for. Align my heart, mind, and desires so they are in line with Yours. For I know that as You do so, my "sadness will develop into gladness." My joy will overflow its banks. In Your precious name, I pray, amen.

JOY GIVER

Lord God of all, powerful Lord, who is like You? All around You we see how faithful You are. You rule over the rising sea. When its waves rise, You quiet them. . . . You have a strong arm. Your hand is powerful. . . . Your throne stands on what is right and fair. Loving-kindness and truth go before You. How happy are the people who know the sound of joy!
PSALM 89:8–9, 13–15 NLV

I'm amazed, Lord, at how faithful You are to me. Especially when I have erred, slipped up, or been unfaithful to You. Thank You, God, that You are in control of not just *my* life but everyone's life, as well as this world's ebb and flow. That gives me hope, Lord. And hope opens the door to joy—not just for me but for everyone, everything, all that You have created. Nothing can overpower You, Lord. So I'm clinging to You. I'm waiting for You, Your justice, Your peace, Your favor, Your strength, Your saving grace. And as I wait, I'm going to trust in You, my joy giver. For in You is goodness. In You is calm. In You, I'm sound and saved. Amen.

THE MORNING STAR RISES

We have the prophetic word. . . . You will do well to pay close attention to it as to a lamp shining in a dismal (squalid and dark) place, until the day breaks through [the gloom] and the Morning Star rises (comes into being) in your hearts. . . . I waited patiently and expectantly for the Lord. . . . [She proudly said] I am my beloved's, and his desire is toward me! . . . Come, my beloved!
2 Peter 1:19; Psalm 40:1; Song of Solomon 7:10–11 ampc

Be with me, Lord Jesus, as I enter Your Word. Help me not just to read it but to take it in, absorb it, and allow it to work its way into my life. Let the light and power of Your Word break through the gloom within me until You rise up and come into being within my heart, changing whatever sorrows that linger into joy. You are my bright morning star, Jesus. For You I patiently wait. It is Your presence I expect to change me from the inside out, letter by letter, word by word. You are my beloved. Desire me as I desire You. Come, Jesus; come now. Amen.

JOY MAKERS

*We who are strong [in our convictions and of robust faith] ought to
bear with the failings and the frailties and the tender scruples of the
weak; [we ought to help carry the doubts and qualms of others] and
not to please ourselves. Let each one of us make it a practice to please
(make happy) his neighbor for his good and for his true welfare,
to edify him [to strengthen him and build him up spiritually].*
ROMANS 15:1–2 AMPC

Lord, I feel so blessed to be aware of the role that joy plays in my life.
But this joy is not just for me alone. This joy is something I can use to
help others. So each day, Lord, as I hope in You, count my blessings,
and revel in the joy of You, remind me to help others, those who are
not as strong in their faith. Help me to please You by helping to
please them, to make them happy, to bring a smile to their faces, to
encourage them, to build them up in their spirits. In other words, Lord,
use me to spread Your joy, from here to eternity! In Jesus' name, I pray,
amen.

TRUE HAPPINESS

Then Haman went out that day glad and with joy in his heart. But when he saw Mordecai at the king's gate, and when he did not stand up or show any fear in front of him, Haman was filled with anger. . . . For the Jews it was a time of joy and happiness and honor. In every part of the nation and in every city where the king's law had come, there was happiness and joy for the Jews.
ESTHER 5:9; 8:16–17 NLV

It's interesting, Lord, how I need to be sure of my source of joy. Does the joy I find in my life come from the deep well of knowing You, seeking You, and abiding in You? Or does my joy come from the shallow stream that eddies around my self-pride, honor, and worldly ambitions? The test seems to be that if my joy comes from the deep well of pleasing You instead of the shallow stream of pleasing myself and the world, my happiness will not be fleeting but a deep, constant, and abiding joy. Help me to seek my joy and happiness in You alone, Lord. For then I will find the everlasting gladness that comes only by living for and in You. Amen.

JOY *in the* JOURNEY

Everything that was written in the Holy Writings long ago was written to teach us. By not giving up, God's Word gives us strength and hope. Now the God Who helps you not to give up and gives you strength will help you think so you can please each other as Christ Jesus did. Then all of you together can thank the God and Father of our Lord Jesus Christ.
ROMANS 15:4–6 NLV

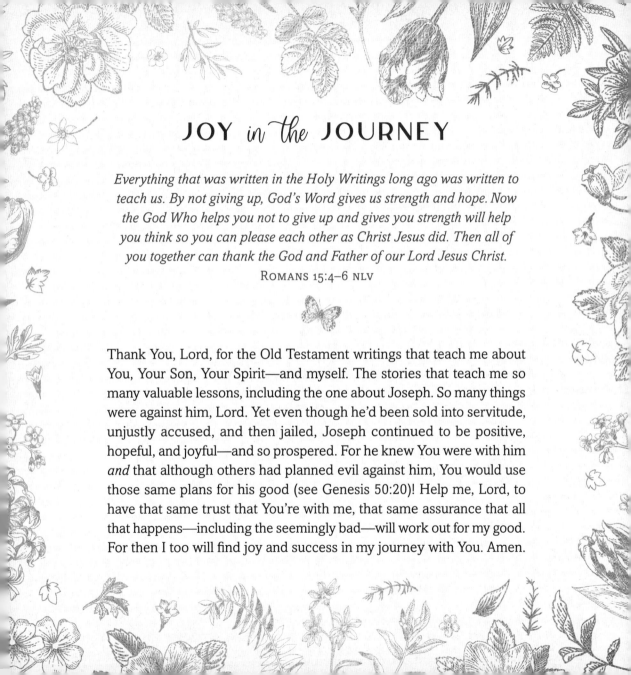

Thank You, Lord, for the Old Testament writings that teach me about You, Your Son, Your Spirit—and myself. The stories that teach me so many valuable lessons, including the one about Joseph. So many things were against him, Lord. Yet even though he'd been sold into servitude, unjustly accused, and then jailed, Joseph continued to be positive, hopeful, and joyful—and so prospered. For he knew You were with him *and* that although others had planned evil against him, You would use those same plans for his good (see Genesis 50:20)! Help me, Lord, to have that same trust that You're with me, that same assurance that all that happens—including the seemingly bad—will work out for my good. For then I too will find joy and success in my journey with You. Amen.

JOY *in the* CHALLENGE

*Peter answered Him, Lord, if it is You, command me to come
to You on the water. He said, Come! So Peter got out of the
boat and walked on the water, and he came toward Jesus. But
when he perceived and felt the strong wind, he was frightened,
and as he began to sink, he cried out, Lord, save me [from death]!
Instantly Jesus reached out His hand and caught and held him.*
MATTHEW 14:28–31 AMPC

You, Jesus, have a way of taking Your followers out of their comfort
zones. First, You direct Your disciples to cross the sea. The next thing
they know, they're desperately trying to ride out a storm. Yet before
they even cry out for help, You appear in a miraculous way, walking
on the water. You yell over their screams, telling them to be brave.
Peter then takes another challenge and begins to walk toward You.
But seeing the wind and waves, he cries out to You—and immediately You grab hold of him. You, Lord, are the joy I find in all my
challenges. With my eyes on You, I can do all things, knowing You'll
be ready to catch me. Amen.

CONSTANT CONVERSATION

*Many, O Lord my God, are the wonderful works which You have
done, and Your thoughts toward us; no one can compare with
You! If I should declare and speak of them, they are too many to
be numbered. . . . I delight to do Your will, O my God; yes, Your
law is within my heart. . . . Let all those that seek and require
You rejoice and be glad in You. . .my Help and my Deliverer.*
PSALM 40:5, 8, 16–17 AMPC

I don't just want You, Lord, but I seek You out, wherever I am, whatever
I'm doing. I'm in constant conversation with You because I need You
more than anything else in this world and the next. There is no greater
guide than You. No greater power, force, refuge, strengthener. You don't
just help me, Lord; You deliver me. You get me out of so many sticky
situations, often ones that I myself have made. Make me ever more
aware of Your presence and my need for You, Lord. In You I find all the
joy I could ever hope for or imagine. In Jesus' name, amen.

FOREVER PRAYER

"While I have been with [My followers] in the world, I have kept them in the power of Your name. I have kept watch over those You gave Me . . . . But now I come to You, Father. I say these things while I am in the world. In this way, My followers may have My joy in their hearts. . . . I do not pray for these followers only. I pray for those who will put their trust in Me."
JOHN 17:12–13, 20 NLV

At times, Jesus, I don't feel very loved or even lovable. I feel unprotected, alone. And then, with all the strength I can muster, I turn to You. I open Your Word. And there I find the comfort, love, safety, and joy I long for. For You, Lord, are watching over me. You keep me safe in the power of God's name. And before You gave up Your life for mine, You even *prayed* to God for *me*! I am one who lives with her trust in You. And this prayer You prayed for me is still rising up with the smoke of incense in the presence of God from the hand of the angel (see Revelation 8:4). I'm overwhelmed, Lord, with joy from and in You, my forever Prayer. Amen.

PROTECTING ANGELS

*He who dwells in the secret place of the Most High shall remain
stable and fixed under the shadow of the Almighty [Whose power
no foe can withstand]. I will say of the Lord, He is my Refuge
and my Fortress, my God; on Him I lean and rely, and in Him
I [confidently] trust! . . . He will cover you. . . . You shall not be
afraid. . . . He will give His angels [especial] charge over you.*
PSALM 91:1–2, 4–5, 11 AMPC

When I'm not trusting You, Lord, worry and dread take all the joy out
of my life. So when I'm in that dark place of fretting and fearing, lift
me up to that secret place—Your presence. Only there will I find the
safety and courage I need! For when I'm in that place, nothing—within
or without—can withstand Your power. Lord, my refuge and fortress,
on You alone I'm leaning and relying. In You I'm putting all my trust.
In You alone do I gain the strength and courage I need to face the day
and find the joy that comes from knowing Your angels are watching
over me. So be it—amen!

ENCAMPED *in* HOPE

I saw the Lord constantly before me, for He is at my right hand that I may not be shaken or overthrown or cast down [from my secure and happy state]. Therefore my heart rejoiced and my tongue exulted exceedingly; moreover, my flesh also will dwell in hope [will encamp, pitch its tent, and dwell in hope]. . . . You have made known to me the ways of life; You will enrapture me [diffusing my soul with joy] with and in Your presence.
ACTS 2:25–26, 28 AMPC

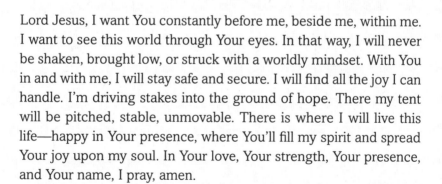

Lord Jesus, I want You constantly before me, beside me, within me. I want to see this world through Your eyes. In that way, I will never be shaken, brought low, or struck with a worldly mindset. With You in and with me, I will stay safe and secure. I will find all the joy I can handle. I'm driving stakes into the ground of hope. There my tent will be pitched, stable, unmovable. There is where I will live this life—happy in Your presence, where You'll fill my spirit and spread Your joy upon my soul. In Your love, Your strength, Your presence, and Your name, I pray, amen.

A STORY to GLORY

What a beautiful thing, GOD, to give thanks, to sing an anthem to you, the High God! To announce your love each daybreak, sing your faithful presence all through the night. . . . You made me so happy, GOD. I saw your work and I shouted for joy. . . . My ears are filled with the sounds of promise: "Good people will prosper. . . . They'll grow tall in the presence of God, lithe and green, virile still in old age."
PSALM 92:1–2, 4, 11–14 MSG

When the world tries to drag me down into hopelessness, I'm going to fight back. I'm going to give thanks to You, Lord. I'm going to sing Your praises, proclaim how much You love me. I'm going to keep You with me throughout the day and then sing about how faithful You are to me at night. All my joy and happiness are bound up in Your promises and presence. As I look around me and see all the wonders You have created, I'll shout for joy. I'll revel in wonder. I'll grow tall in Your garden and continue to be productive even when I'm old. May I be a story reflecting Your glory. In Jesus' name, amen.

REJOICING *on the* WAY

*An angel of the Lord said to Philip, "Rise and go.". . . And he rose
and went. . . . The Spirit said to Philip, "Go over and join this chariot."
So Philip ran to [the eunuch]. . . . And [Philip] baptized him. And when
they came up out of the water, the Spirit of the Lord carried Philip
away, and the eunuch saw him no more, and went on his way rejoicing.*
ACTS 8:26–27, 29–30, 38–39 ESV

Lord, I love living in Your Word, experiencing Your joy, growing in
my faith. But You want me to do more. You want me to share You
with others so that they too can experience all those things, all those
blessings in, with, and from You. So today, Lord, I pray that You would
keep me ever attentive to Your direction. That You would open my
ears to the voice of Your Spirit. And that once I hear that voice, You
would enable me to go where the Spirit wants me to go, do what He
wants me to do, and say what He wants me to say so that others can
go on Your way rejoicing. In Jesus' name, I pray, amen.

THE RIGHT WAY *to* JOY

To do what is right and good and fair is more pleasing to the Lord than gifts given on the altar in worship. . . . When what is right and fair is done, it is a joy for those who are right with God. . . . He who follows what is right and loving and kind finds life, right-standing with God and honor. . . . The horse is made ready for war, but winning the fight belongs to the Lord.

PROVERBS 21:3, 15, 21, 31 NLV

Lord, sometimes I just don't understand this world. So many people think they hold the right answers, yet those answers are not of You. They don't jive with what You would have Your followers be and do. Yet the "right people" who appear to be "wrong in You" seem to be increasing. Justice seems to be the golden ring society rarely obtains. So I'm looking to You, Lord. Help me do what is right, good, and fair in Your eyes. Give me the strength to please You alone, despite the people pleasers who surround me. Help me to follow the good way, the right path, *Your* path, leaving the results to You. For only then will I find joy the "right" way. Amen.

FROM DAWN *to* DUSK

He spread a cloud for a covering, and fire to give light at night.
They asked, and He brought them quails for meat. And He filled them
with the bread of heaven. He opened the rock and water flowed out.
It flowed in the desert like a river. For He remembered His holy Word. . . .
He brought His people out with joy, His chosen ones with singing.
PSALM 105:39–43 NLV

When I need to hide, Lord, You protect me, covering me with a cloud.
When I am walking in darkness, in the deep shadows of night, You
provide a fire to give light. When I ask for food, when I thirst for water,
You provide both in abundance. You remember Your promises and
You keep Your word. All the ways You take care of me are more than
I can fathom, Lord. Be with me once more this day, from the time I
begin my work for You until the moment I lay down my head. Bring
me through, Lord, with joy. May my last thoughts be songs of praise
to You. In Jesus' name, amen.

FREEDOM *in* JOY

Peter was held in prison. But the church kept praying to God for
him. . . . Peter was sleeping between two soldiers. . . . The angel
hit Peter on the side and said, "Get up!" Then the chains fell off
his hands. . . . He went to Mary's house . . . . Peter knocked at the
gate. . . . In her joy [Rhoda] forgot to open the gate. She ran in
and told them that Peter was standing outside.

ACTS 12:5–7, 12–14 NLV

The joy of answered prayer! The joy in knowing we have access to You.
The happiness in the knowledge that we can come to You, give You
our heartfelt concerns, and know You have heard us and will act on our
behalf. The power You exude in response—reaching across time and
space, sending down Your angels, and having them work out Your will in
Your way as You free us, our family, our friends, and total strangers from
the constraints that bind us. Lord, thank You for hearing our prayers. For
moving on our behalf. For the answers You provide, ones that defy all
expectations and imaginations, and leave us overcome with joy. Amen.

TWO THINGS. . .

Two things I have asked of You. . . . Take lies and what is false far
from me. Do not let me be poor or rich. Feed me with the food that
I need. Then I will not be afraid that I will be full and turn my back
against You and say, "Who is the Lord?" And I will not be afraid that
I will be poor and steal, and bring shame on the name of my God.
PROVERBS 30:7–9 NLV

Two things that steal joy, Lord: getting caught in a snare of lies and
living in a state of discontentment. So I bring You this prayer. First,
Lord, please give me the courage to be honest. For all lies are against
You, the God of truth. Second, Lord, please grant me enough to
live on—no more, no less. Not more because I don't want "stuff"—
possessions, treasures on earth—to come between me and You. Yet
not less so that I won't have to depend on others or be tempted to take
from others and bring disgrace to me and You. That's it, Lord. The
truth and enough to get by. That will be all I need to gain, maintain,
and proclaim my joy in You! In Jesus' name, I pray, amen.

GOOD THINGS

*Some traveled through the desert wastes. They did not find a
way. . . . Their souls became weak within them. Then they cried
out to the Lord in their trouble. And He took them out of their
suffering. He led them by a straight path. . . . He fills the thirsty
soul. And He fills the hungry soul with good things. . . . Let them
give Him gifts of thanks and tell of His works with songs of joy.*
PSALM 107:4–7, 9, 22 NLV

So often, Lord, I find myself just wandering. I cannot find my way in,
out, over, around, under, or through. And as I go on wandering, my soul
grows weak within me. Then I look up. I cry to You, longing to see Your
face. And You come quickly. You lift me up, turn me around, show me
the right way to go. As I follow Your directions, I see glimpses of You
out ahead of me, beckoning, encouraging, loving. And in the resting
places, You quench my thirsty and hungering soul with good—all that I
need to thrive, to continue on with You. It is for this and so much more
that I sing a song of praise and joy to You, the God of my life. Amen.

POWER RELEASED

He, having received [so strict a] charge, put them into the inner prison (the dungeon) and fastened their feet in the stocks. But about midnight, as Paul and Silas were praying and singing hymns of praise to God, and the [other] prisoners were listening to them, suddenly there was a great earthquake, so that the very foundations of the prison were shaken; and at once all the doors were opened and everyone's shackles were unfastened.
ACTS 16:24–26 AMPC

It's true, Lord, that sometimes joy leads me into praising You. But oftentimes, I find that even when joy seems elusive, when I just can't get there from where I am, praise pulls my heart out of the darkness and my mind off its troubles and brings me right smack into joy! So here I am, Lord, coming to You chained by my sorrow, my mood, my darkness. I'm raising my voice in praise and song to You. And as I do, as my words leave my lips and rise up to Your ears, I find Your power unleashed. The foundation of my troubles, worries, and what-ifs is shaken to its core! And all at once, my door to You, to joy, is opened. I'm free of my shackles! Thank You for releasing me and pulling me up into You! Amen!

INTO HIS KEEPING

[The jailer]. . .fell down before Paul and Silas. . . . Men, what is it
necessary for me to do that I may be saved? And they answered,
Believe in the Lord Jesus Christ [give yourself up to Him, take
yourself out of your own keeping and entrust yourself into His
keeping] and you will be saved, [and this applies both to] you and
your household as well. . . . Then he. . .leaped much for joy.
ACTS 16:29–31, 34 AMPC

So often, Lord, I find that I really haven't given You all of me. I attempt to take care of myself, to trust my own skills, resources, and knowledge. I actually think I know better than You! Today, Jesus, make me a woman totally in Your keeping. Help me to give You all of me, to leave nothing behind. To entrust all things to You—my mind, body, soul, spirit, family, friends, country, possessions, present, and future. Remind me of Your power, grace, forgiveness, and wisdom. Help me to get it through my head that only by taking myself out of my own keeping and into Yours will I find the joy that will make me want to leap, to dance, to sing in Your name. Amen.

HOME ONCE MORE

Some sat in darkness and in the shadow of death. They suffered in prison in iron chains. Because they had turned against the Words of God. . . . Then they cried out to the Lord in their trouble. And He saved them. . . . He brought them out of darkness and the shadow of death. And He broke their chains. . . . Let them give Him gifts of thanks and tell of His works with songs of joy.
PSALM 107:10–11, 13–14, 22 NLV

Even when I go against Your Word, Lord, You save me. Even when my own stubbornness leads me away from Your will and toward my own, You hear my cry. When all around is darkness, You bring me back out into the light of Your way. You break the ties that have bound me. And once again I am humbled. I can barely look up at You. For although I am full of joy that I am back in Your light, I am full of shame. Why am I so willful? Forgive me, Lord. Pull me into Your compassionate embrace. Hold me tight as I snuggle back into Your warmth, so glad to be home with You once more. Amen.

WORD WELCOMED

They answered, Believe in the Lord Jesus Christ. . . . And they declared the Word of the Lord. . . . And he took them the same hour of the night and bathed [them because of their bloody] wounds. . . . Then he took them up into his house and set food before them; and he leaped much for joy and exulted with all his family that he believed in God [accepting and joyously welcoming what He had made known through Christ].

ACTS 16:31–34 AMPC

Oh gentlest of Saviors, how much You still have to teach me. I *do* believe in You. I put myself entirely in Your keeping, leaving no remainder behind to fret or fear. And then I read Your Word, and my eyes are opened. My heart moved. Your gentleness prompts me to be gentle to others—the chained, injured, and lost. To pull them close to me and to tend to their wounds. To share what I have with them. For as Your Word fills every crevice of want and desire, I am led to You, Your power, Your grace, Your love, and Your light, which then flow through me and onto others. Your Word is more than welcome in my life, Lord. It *is* my life. Amen.

ENJOYING *the* DAYS

I know that it will be well for those who fear God. . . . But it will not go well for the sinful. . . . There are right and good men who have the same thing happen to them that happens to those who do sinful things. And there are sinful men who have the same thing happen to them that happens to those who are right and good. . . . So I say a man should enjoy himself. . . . Eat and drink and be happy. . . through the days. . .which God has given him.

ECCLESIASTES 8:12–15 NLV

I keep waiting, Lord, for bad people to "get theirs." But they never seem to! And Your Word says that's just how it is. Sometimes bad things happen to good people, and good things happen to bad people. At least on earth, anyway. So help me, Lord, to turn all these thoughts over to You. To realize I'll never be able to figure everything out, but You have, and You will take care of it. Meanwhile, I'm going to enjoy my days with You right here, right now. I'm going to live and be joy filled in Your name. Amen!

HEAVENLY DEW

You will guard him and keep him in perfect and constant peace whose mind [both its inclination and its character] is stayed on You, because he commits himself to You, leans on You, and hopes confidently in You. So trust in the Lord (commit yourself to Him, lean on Him, hope confidently in Him) forever. . . . You who dwell in the dust, awake and sing for joy! For Your dew [O Lord] is a dew of [sparkling] light [heavenly, supernatural dew].

ISAIAH 26:3–4, 19 AMPC

I'm keeping my mind, heart, soul, and spirit focused on You, Lord. For when I do, Your guard of peace comes up all around me. Its shield keeps me still within, no matter what is happening without. In You I find my refuge, for to You alone I am committed. On You alone I lean. All my hope and expectation lie in You—not just today, in this moment on earth, but forever. Beyond this day and all the days to come. Rain down Your love upon me, Lord. For it's Your refreshment that keeps me from running dry and in the current of Your presence and all the love and joy that come with it. Amen.

A LODE *of* JOY

In all our affliction, I am overflowing with joy. For even when we came into Macedonia, our bodies had no rest, but we were afflicted at every turn—fighting without and fear within. But God, who comforts the downcast, comforted us by the coming of Titus, and not only by his coming but also by the comfort with which he was comforted by you. . .so that I rejoiced still more.

2 CORINTHIANS 7:4–7 ESV

It's amazing, Lord, how contagious our emotions can be! What I express has an effect on all those around me! So help me, Lord, to overflow with joy—no matter what is going on in my life. To find and tap into that deep, abiding lode of spiritual joy You have waiting for me, streaming just beneath the surface. For as You comfort me and fill me with gladness, my friends, family, coworkers, and even complete strangers will find themselves eased in their own pain and affliction. Our fighting without and fears within will dissipate and become as nothing but fool's gold, something that is easily thrown away as we treasure what we have in You! Amen!

EAGERLY AWAITING

I bore you on eagles' wings and brought you to Myself. . . .
The eternal God is your refuge and dwelling place, and underneath
are the everlasting arms. . . . [Looking forward to the shepherd's
arrival, the eager girl pictures their meeting and says]. . .Oh, that his
left hand were under my head and that his right hand embraced me!
. . . Let all those that seek and require You rejoice and be glad in You.
Exodus 19:4; Deuteronomy 33:27; Song of Solomon 8:1, 3; Psalm
40:16 AMPC

Lord, thank You for hovering over me. For bearing me on eagles' wings,
bringing me out of myself and into You. You are my refuge. In You I
live, move, and have my being. You hold me up when I'm down. You
turn my life around. Each and every morning, I look for You, eagerly
anticipating the calm, peace, love, and joy I'll experience when Your
left hand gently cradles my head and Your right hand draws me into
You. Come, Lord. I'm waiting. I'm willing and ready to melt into Your
love and affection. In Jesus' name, I pray, amen.

A JOYFUL WALK *with* JESUS

I am going. . .bound by the [Holy] Spirit and obligated and compelled
by the [convictions of my own] spirit, not knowing what will befall
me. . . except that the Holy Spirit clearly and emphatically affirms
to me. . .that imprisonment and suffering await me. But none of
these things move me; neither do I esteem my life dear to myself, if
only I may finish my course with joy and the ministry which I have
obtained from [which was entrusted to me by] the Lord Jesus.
ACTS 20:22–24 AMPC

I'm not really sure what lies before me, Lord. Only You can see all things
that have been, are, and will be. But I know that Your Spirit is leading
my spirit, urging me to move ahead, to continue on with the gifts You
have given me, in the direction You have sent me. Whatever happens,
good or bad, doesn't really matter to me. The only desire I have is to
finish my walk with You with joy, working where and when You allow.
Thank You, Lord, for making me a part of Your plan. In Jesus' name,
I pray, amen.

HEALING WORD

Some were fools because of their wrong-doing. They had troubles because of their sins. . . . And they came near the gates of death. Then they cried out to the Lord in their trouble. And He saved them from their suffering. He sent His Word and healed them. And He saved them from the grave. . . . Let them give Him gifts of thanks and tell of His works with songs of joy.
PSALM 107:17–20, 22 NLV

Whenever I miss the target You've set for me, Lord, trouble follows. Only then, it seems, do I stop and regret the things I said or did. Only then do I cry out for You to save me from the consequences of my sin. And even then, in those times when I'm not proud of myself in any way, shape, or form, You come when I call. You save me, pull me out, lift me up, restore me. You send Your Word to heal me. You give me life once more. There is no way I can ever repay all You do for me, Lord. All I can offer is my humble thanks and songs of joy, love, and gratitude. Amen.

OPEN *to* JOY

Give strength to weak hands and to weak knees. Say to those whose heart is afraid, "Have strength of heart, and do not be afraid. See, your God will come. . . . He will save you." Then the eyes of the blind will be opened. And the ears of those who cannot hear will be opened. Then those who cannot walk will jump like a deer. And the tongue of those who cannot speak will call out for joy.
ISAIAH 35:3–6 NLV

Your Word, Lord—oh, how it feeds every part of me! It gives strength, power, and energy to my weak hands and knees. Your Word swells my heart, filling it with the courage I need to face things I'd rather not face, things I can overcome only when You stand with me. Your Word opens the eyes of my heart each time I look within its pages. Your voice reveals new meanings, helping me to understand things that were once cloudy. You make me want to leap and shout for joy! Continue with me, Lord. Today reveal the wonder and power of Your Word until my soul once again rejoices. Amen.

GIVING FIRST *to* GOD

*[The Macedonian churches] have been put to the test by much trouble,
but they have much joy. They have given much even though they were
very poor. They gave as much as they could because they wanted to. They
asked from their hearts if they could help the Christians in Jerusalem.
It was more than we expected. They gave themselves to the Lord first.
Then they gave themselves to us to be used as the Lord wanted.*

2 CORINTHIANS 8:2–5 NLV

There is such joy in giving, Lord. But there are so many worthy causes.
It can be difficult to know which to choose. So, Lord, make Your desires
clear to me. As I give myself first to You, I'm relying on You to help
me to home in on the causes You want me to support through service,
provisions, or money. Lord, I want to give from the heart and soul. And
after I do, I'm not going to worry about where my next dollar will be
coming from but will rely on You to provide for me as I help provide for
others—with absolute joy and pleasure. In Jesus' name, amen.

A JOYFUL COMEBACK

"Come back to me and really mean it!" . . . Change your life,
not just your clothes. Come back to GOD, your God. And here's
why: God is kind and merciful. He takes a deep breath, puts up
with a lot, this most patient God, extravagant in love, always
ready to cancel catastrophe. Who knows? Maybe he'll do it now,
maybe he'll turn around and show pity. Maybe, when all's said
and done, there'll be blessings full and robust for your GOD!
JOEL 2:12–14 MSG

Lord, I know sometimes I'm just not there for You. Not like You're always here for me. I've gotten so busy living life, I've forgotten to live it for You! As a result, all joy seems to have gone out of me. So forgive me, God, for wandering away. I know You are kind, loving, and compassionate. You have so much more love for me than I do for myself right now, Lord. So let's change things up. As I come back to You, Lord, come back to me. Turn my life around to the good. Shower Your blessings upon me as I joyfully await Your power and presence in my life once more! In Jesus' name, amen.

FREEDOM *to* CHOOSE

You were chosen to be free. Be careful that you do not please your old selves by sinning because you are free. Live this free life by loving and helping others. . . . Let the Holy Spirit lead you in each step. Then you will not please your sinful old selves. . . . The fruit that comes from having the Holy Spirit in our lives is: love, joy, peace, not giving up, being kind, being good, having faith, being gentle, and being the boss over our own desires.

GALATIANS 5:13, 16, 22–23 NLV

Your Word, Lord, makes it clear that You *chose* me to be free! For that privilege I praise You, Lord. Yet I don't want that same freedom to lead me to please myself. I want to please *You*. And the only way to do that is by letting Your Holy Spirit lead me in every way, every day. So help me, Lord, to keep close to You. To home in on what the Holy Spirit would have me do, where He would have me go. Then I will have the love, joy, peace, and so much more that comes from walking in Your will and way! In Jesus' name, I pray, amen.

REGAINING STRENGTH

Let them give Him gifts of thanks and tell of His works with songs of joy. Some went out to sea in ships. . . . He spoke and raised up a storm. . . . Their strength of heart left them in their danger. . . . They did not know what to do. Then they cried out to the Lord in their trouble. And He took them out of all their problems. He stopped the storm, and the waves of the sea became quiet. Then they were glad because the sea became quiet. And He led them to the safe place they wanted.

PSALM 107:22–23, 25–30 NLV

When I go out on my own, I usually end up exhausted just when I need the most strength. That's when I finally realize I've left You out of my boat, Lord. I cry to You, and You come to my rescue. You stop the wind and the waves. In the quiet, I hear Your voice. I'm overwhelmed with gladness. My heart regains strength. And You lead me to the exact place I'd been heading all along. Thank You, Lord, for always being there for me, helping me, rescuing me, delivering me. Amen.

THIRSTING *for* GOD'S VOICE

Wait and listen, everyone who is thirsty! Come to the waters; and he who has no money, come, buy and eat! Yes, come, buy [priceless, spiritual] wine and milk without money and without price [simply for the self-surrender that accepts the blessing]. Why do you spend your money for that which is not bread, and your earnings for what does not satisfy? Hearken diligently to Me, and eat what is good, and let your soul delight itself in fatness [the profuseness of spiritual joy].
ISAIAH 55:1–2 AMPC

Lord, I am so ready to drink from Your well of wisdom. There are so many voices out there, telling me what is right and what is wrong, what I should do and what I shouldn't do. Help me, Lord, to silence the words—written and spoken—of others that are ringing through my head. Give me the power and strength to focus on Yours alone. What You have within Your Book is the wisdom I crave. Show me what You would have me read. Then open the doors of my mind so that I can comprehend what You're telling me. Give my soul the joy and delight of Your direction! In Jesus' name, I pray, amen.

MIND EXCHANGE

Incline your ear [submit and consent to the divine will] and come to Me; hear, and your soul will revive. . . . Seek, inquire for, and require the Lord while He may be found [claiming Him by necessity and by right]; call upon Him while He is near. . . . For My thoughts are not your thoughts, neither are your ways My ways, says the Lord. . . . You shall go out. . .with joy and be led forth [by your Leader, the Lord Himself, and His word] with peace.
ISAIAH 55:3, 6, 8, 12 AMPC

Help me to readjust my ears so that I can pick up on Your wavelength, Lord. I'm drawing near to You, waiting and wanting to hear what You have to say. Refresh my soul, Lord, with Your Word as I seek Your face while You're so near to me. I'm calling out to You, emptying my own mind of its constant dialogue so that I can actually *hear* Your voice and exchange my thoughts for Yours, which are always so far above me yet penetrate deep into my own heart. For when I tap into Your wisdom and love, I find myself tasting Your joy and being led, not just by Your peace, but by You Yourself! Amen.

ROOTS IN REALITY

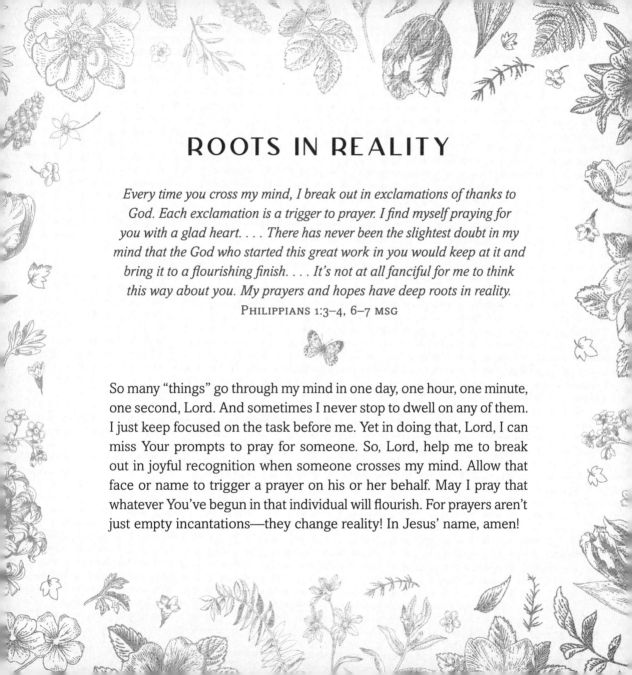

Every time you cross my mind, I break out in exclamations of thanks to God. Each exclamation is a trigger to prayer. I find myself praying for you with a glad heart. . . . There has never been the slightest doubt in my mind that the God who started this great work in you would keep at it and bring it to a flourishing finish. . . . It's not at all fanciful for me to think this way about you. My prayers and hopes have deep roots in reality.
PHILIPPIANS 1:3–4, 6–7 MSG

So many "things" go through my mind in one day, one hour, one minute, one second, Lord. And sometimes I never stop to dwell on any of them. I just keep focused on the task before me. Yet in doing that, Lord, I can miss Your prompts to pray for someone. So, Lord, help me to break out in joyful recognition when someone crosses my mind. Allow that face or name to trigger a prayer on his or her behalf. May I pray that whatever You've begun in that individual will flourish. For prayers aren't just empty incantations—they change reality! In Jesus' name, amen!

HAPPY IN FAITH

Because of your prayers and the help the Holy Spirit gives me,
all of this will turn out for good. . . . To me, living means having
Christ. To die means that I would have more of Him. If I keep on
living here in this body, it means that I can lead more people to
Christ. . . . I have a desire to leave this world to be with Christ,
which is much better. But it is more important for you that I stay.
I am sure I will live to help you grow and be happy in your faith.
PHILIPPIANS 1:19, 21–25 NLV

Some days, Lord, life can be so hard that I just want You to beam me
up. To lift up every part of me into heaven with You. Yet I know You
have plans for me that are for my good and Your purpose. So help
me to be happy wherever I am, Lord, in heaven or on earth. Remind
me that things will, in the end, always turn out for good. Show me,
Lord, whom You would have me help and whom You would have
me lead to You so they can find joy in You. I live to serve You, Lord.
In Jesus' name, amen.

THAT MIDDLE GROUND

*If any person thinks himself to be somebody [too important to condescend
to shoulder another's load] when he is nobody [of superiority except
in his own estimation], he deceives and deludes and cheats himself.
But let every person carefully scrutinize and examine and test his
own conduct and his own work. He can then have the personal
satisfaction and joy of doing something commendable [in itself alone]
without [resorting to] boastful comparison with his neighbor.*
GALATIANS 6:3–4 AMPC

Lord, too often I find myself comparing my work with that of others.
And then I find myself in one of two places: I'm either not satisfied or
too satisfied with what I've accomplished. If it's the former, I begin to
feel less worthy, less able, less competent. In other words, I feel less
than who You've made me to be. If it's the latter, I find myself feeling
too worthy, too capable, and too self-sufficient. Then before I know it,
pride has set in. Help me, Lord, to find that middle ground. To know
that my joy lies in comparing myself with myself and in doing my work
for and in You. That is my soul reward. In Jesus' name, amen.

SPROUTING WITH HOPE

*He changes a desert into a pool of water and makes water flow out
of dry ground. And He makes the hungry go there. . . . They plant
seeds in the fields and plant grape-vines and gather much fruit.
He lets good come to them and they become many in number. . . .
He lifts those in need out of their troubles. He makes their families
grow like flocks. Those who are right see it and are glad.*
<small>PSALM 107:35–38, 41–42 NLV</small>

When I'm in a place that seems dry of hope, Lord, I pray to You, and You
make water appear out of nowhere. Soon that once-barren landscape
within begins to come back to life. You open my eyes to what may be.
You urge me to plant seeds of confidence and expectation in You. And
soon I'm bearing more fruit than I ever hoped or imagined. Good things
begin to sprout up, feeding every part of me—mind, body, spirit, and soul.
Once again, Lord, You lift me up out of myself and into You. And I am
overcome with gladness, singing with joy. Thank You, Lord, for bringing
me back to where You want me to be—joyfully expectant in You. Amen.

THE WE-TRAIN

Are you strong because you belong to Christ? Does His love comfort you?
Do you have joy by being as one in sharing the Holy Spirit? Do you have
loving-kindness and pity for each other? Then give me true joy by thinking
the same thoughts. Keep having the same love. Be as one in thoughts and
actions. . . . Think of other people as more important than yourself.
PHILIPPIANS 2:1–3 NLV

Lord, I'm back on that all-about-me train. How do I keep getting stuck here? It never leads to happiness, that's for sure. Help me, Lord, to realize that my strength lies is putting others before myself and finding that my joy is tied up with *their* joy. So lead me today, Lord, to be more others- than self-focused. To keep my eyes open to where I can lend a hand or to whom I can lend an ear. Show me to whom You would have me extend a hand of friendship or a word of love. Instead of finding where I am different from another, show me where she and I are the same and can find common ground. Help me to get on the we-train and embark upon a joy-meets-joy journey. In Jesus' name, I pray, amen.

POWER OF THE WORD

The rain and snow come down from heaven and do not return there without giving water to the earth. This makes plants grow on the earth, and gives seeds to the planter and bread to the eater. So My Word which goes from My mouth will not return to Me empty. It will do what I want it to do, and will carry out My plan well. You will go out with joy, and be led out in peace.

ISAIAH 55:10–12 NLV

The power of Your Word, Lord, is astounding. Just as the rain and snow You send to earth promote growth for the fields and food for the farmer, so does Your Word provide growth and sustenance in my life. It is food for my soul and water for my spirit. Your Word carries out Your plan for me and all Your children. Your promises, so much stronger than my good intentions, grow me into the person You want and *need* me to be so that Your will on earth will be done. In and because of all this, I am on the path of Your joy, led by Your peace. In Jesus' name, amen!

SHORE OF GOD'S DESIRE

When they had rowed three or four miles, they saw Jesus walking on the sea and approaching the boat. And they were afraid (terrified). But Jesus said to them, It is I; be not afraid! [I Am; stop being frightened!] Then they were quite willing and glad for Him to come into the boat. And now the boat went at once to the land they had steered toward. [And immediately they reached the shore toward which they had been slowly making their way.]

JOHN 6:19–21 AMPC

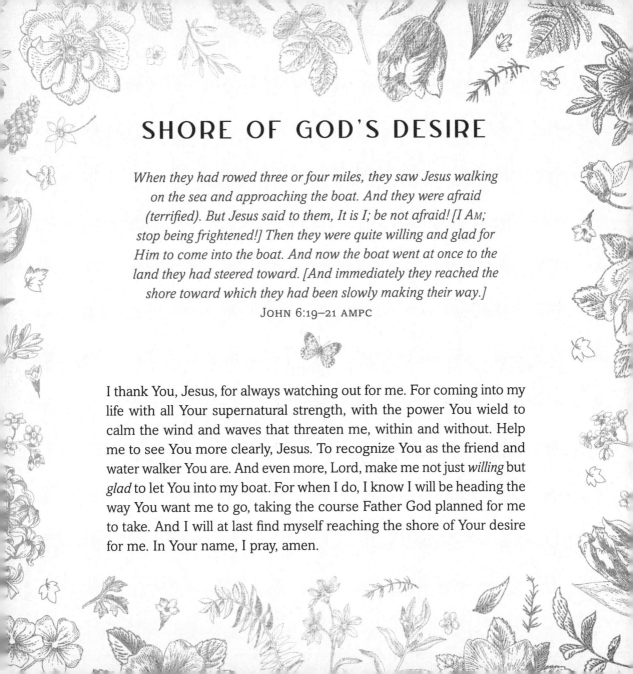

I thank You, Jesus, for always watching out for me. For coming into my life with all Your supernatural strength, with the power You wield to calm the wind and waves that threaten me, within and without. Help me to see You more clearly, Jesus. To recognize You as the friend and water walker You are. And even more, Lord, make me not just *willing* but *glad* to let You into my boat. For when I do, I know I will be heading the way You want me to go, taking the course Father God planned for me to take. And I will at last find myself reaching the shore of Your desire for me. In Your name, I pray, amen.

CHANGE OF PLANS

Do not always be thinking about your own plans only. Be happy to know what other people are doing. Think as Christ Jesus thought. Jesus has always been as God is. But He did not hold to His rights as God. He put aside everything that belonged to Him and made Himself the same as a servant who is owned by someone. . . . He gave up His important place.
PHILIPPIANS 2:4–8 NLV

Sometimes, Lord, I tend to get so wrapped up in my own life and plans that I never look around or show any interest in what's happening in the lives of others. Help me to reach out, Lord. I actually want to listen to the plans, dreams, and callings in the lives of others. Help me to put aside what I'd planned for today, even if it's just for a little while, and show an interest in another's ideas. And especially help me, Lord, to be more gracious amid interruptions, recognizing them not as something keeping me from getting what *I* want done that day but as opportunities to do what *You* would have me do to serve You. In Jesus' name, amen.

JOYFUL AND OBEDIENT

You must keep on working to show you have been saved from the punishment of sin. Be afraid that you may not please God. He is working in you. God is helping you obey Him. God is doing what He wants done in you. Be glad you can do the things you should be doing. Do all things without arguing and talking about how you wish you did not have to do them. In that way, you can prove yourselves to be without blame.
PHILIPPIANS 2:12–15 NLV

Some days I feel like one of the wandering Israelites, Lord. I'm moaning and groaning about all the things I don't want to do. Help me to look at all the blessings in my life instead of at all the seeming curses. For I want to please You, Lord. And no one likes a whiner. Open my eyes to what You are doing within me. Help me not to give up on myself—or You—but recognize that You are helping me follow the path You have purposefully put before me. Make me not stubborn but pliant to Your directions. I want to become the joyful and obedient child You desire, walking in Your way instead of pouting and protesting on the sidelines. In Jesus' name, amen.

A GOOD PLACE

I cried to the Lord in my trouble, and He. . . put me in a good place. The Lord is with me. I will not be afraid of what man can do to me. The Lord is with me. He is my Helper. . .my strength and my song. . .the One Who saves me. The joy of being saved is being heard in the tents of those who are right and good. The right hand of the Lord does powerful things.
PSALM 118:5–7, 14–15 NLV

Lord, I cannot help but sing praises, to be filled with childlike joy! For when I cry out to You, You swoop down and lift me up. You put me in a good place, one where I can catch my breath, see things anew, regain my hope and strength. Because You are with me, I need not fear anything! For You are my helper, my strength, my song. Because Your Son has made me good and right in Your eyes, You will never let me fall. All day long, my joy, my courage, my blessings are met in the mantra, "You, Lord, are with me. You, Lord, are with me." In Jesus' name, amen.

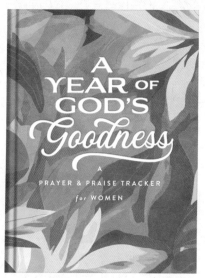